Excel for Windows® 95

Quick & Easy

Third Edition

Gerald E. Jones

SYBEX®

San Francisco Paris Düsseldorf Soest

Acquisitions Manager: Kristine Plachy
Developmental Editor: Richard Mills
Revisor: Michelle Moore
Editors: Doug Robert, Neil Edde
Technical Editor: Sandra Teng
Desktop Publisher: Deborah A. Bevilacqua
Production Assistant: Kim Askew-Qasem
Indexer: Matthew Spence
Cover Designer: Design Site
Cover Illustrator: Jack Meyers

Library of Congress Card Number: 95-71250
ISBN: 0-7821-1783-X

Manufactured in the United States of America
10 9 8 7 6 5 4 3 2 1

Acknowledgments

A team of dedicated professionals worked to develop and produce this book. Special thanks to Michelle Moore, who revised the content for this edition. At SYBEX, thanks to Richard Mills, developmental editor; Doug Robert and Neil Edde, editors; Sandra Teng, technical editor; Deborah Bevilacqua, desktop publisher; and Kim Askew-Qasem, proofreader/production assistant. Special thanks to Peter Nathan, Senior Decision Support Analyst at Paramount Pictures, for suggesting the design of the check register example. And personal thanks, as always, to Georja Oumano Jones, who is a star.

Contents at a Glance

Table of Contents

Contents

LESSON 6

LESSON 7

LESSON 8

Introduction

This book is intended to help you *learn by doing*. Specifically, its subject is Microsoft Excel for Windows 95. But the broader aim of the book is to help you solve practical problems. The focus is on problems in business, the kinds of tasks and assignments that you encounter every day if your job involves financial accounting. Of course, in business, this includes just about everybody. For example, almost everyone has to balance a checkbook or turn in an employee expense report, so these are precisely the tasks that are used as examples in this book. You will create an electronic check register that can generate an ongoing balance, and you will design and print an expense report. These will be fully workable, practical tools that you can use long after you no longer need them as learning aids.

How to Use This Book

You need to have little or no prior knowledge of either Windows or Excel to use this book successfully. In approach, *Excel for Windows 95 Quick & Easy* is a book to be used rather than simply read. It should be on your desk to guide you as you sit at your computer and work through its exercises. Each lesson is a short work session that can be performed in about ten minutes. Each lesson focuses on a set of program features that can be applied to a practical problem—such as balancing a checkbook. Lessons are organized to be done in sequence, though not necessarily all at once. One or two lessons per day is a good pace. If several days pass between lessons, glance back at the previous lesson as a quick review before you continue. The sequence naturally begins with very basic operations and tasks, and makes a logical, step-by-step progression toward more ambitious assignments.

Always try to work through a lesson in its entirety. The procedures prompt you to save your work to disk at the end of each lesson. If, for some reason, you must stop work in the middle of a lesson, *be sure to save your work!* Remember that electronic computer memory is not permanent. If you do not save your work to a disk file, it will be lost when power to the computer is turned off.

There are two fundamental elements to the presentation: *procedural steps* and *visual references*. The procedural steps are numbered computer operations. You will read each step and then perform it using the mouse or keyboard as you work with Excel. Next to many steps, a color picture of the computer screen is shown. This is your visual reference—a snapshot, in effect, of what your screen should look like as you are executing a procedure. With this unique visual approach, you won't go astray. (Or, if you do, you won't go very far astray!)

NOTE
Occasionally, the text will be supplemented with a Note, which may highlight an alternate method, provide a reminder, or alert you to possible difficulties.

Most of the procedures assume that you will be using the mouse to make selections. Keyboard selections usually are described only when pressing a key is the quickest or most natural way to do something.

This book truly aims to deliver on the promise of its title—namely, that learning Excel can be quick and easy. You are not necessarily learning Excel because you enjoy investigating new computer software products. You want the minimum, essential information for getting the job done. Consequently, each session concludes with some functional result, which you will save immediately to disk for your ongoing use. Since each lesson requires only minutes to complete, you can work through the steps whenever you have just a little time—on a coffee break, between phone calls, or perhaps just to get a quick sense of accomplishment before ending your workday.

The Most Basic Skills

Here's a brief summary of basic Windows operations that will help you in any Windows 95 application, not just Excel. For more information about getting around in Windows 95, see *Windows 95 Quick & Easy* (©1995 SYBEX) or *Mastering Windows 95* (©1995 SYBEX).

Making Selections with a Mouse

A *mouse* is a movable device for pointing and making selections on the computer screen. As you move the mouse around on your desktop, a small symbol called a *pointer* moves along with it on the screen. The pointer can change shape to indicate the type of selection being made.

There are three main types of actions that can be performed by pressing the left mouse button:

Clicking: Point to the item you want and press the left button once, briefly.

Double-clicking: Point to the item and click the left button twice rapidly.

Dragging: Point to an item, press and hold down the left button, continue to hold down the button as you move the mouse to a new location, and then release the button. (In the first few lessons of this book, you will sometimes be reminded after a dragging procedure to release the mouse button. However, *drag* always means all three actions: click and hold, move, and release.)

Menu Selections

Commands you can select in Excel appear in a menu bar beneath the title bar of the program window. A window represents a currently running task or open document. The title bar gives the name of the window. The title bar and start-up menu bar of Excel appear at the top of the screen. To make a selection from a menu bar, follow these steps:

1 Click the menu item you want, such as **File**. Or, at the keyboard, press **Alt**, then the underscored letter of the item you want, such as **f**.

2 Select a command, such as **Open**, from the pull-down menu that appears. Click the item with the mouse, or press its underscored letter on the keyboard.

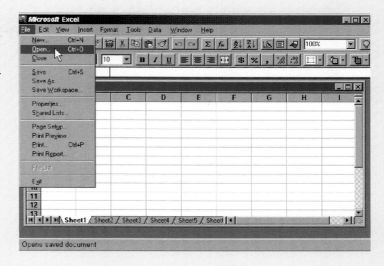

Getting Help

To display a window containing explanatory text on any action within Windows or Excel, press **F1**. You can get a listing of Help topics (or search for specific topics by name) by selecting Help from the menu bar.

Don't let the technicalities here discourage you. You don't need any special knowledge before you start working. If you know how to point and click with the mouse, you have ample preparation. If you can devote a few minutes to working through Lesson 1, you will see for yourself how learning Excel for Windows can be quick and easy!

Getting Acquainted with Worksheets

In this lesson, you will learn about the basic elements of an electronic document called a *worksheet*. A worksheet is simply an accounting-style spreadsheet that can be held in computer memory and stored on disk.

In following the steps below, you will build a type of worksheet you can probably use every day—a check register.

This book is all about learning by doing, so turn on your computer and get started.

> **NOTE**
> The discussion assumes that you are already familiar with simple Windows operations like using the mouse or keyboard to make selections and execute commands from pull-down menus. In this book, procedures that involve a sequence of menu selections are shown with the commands linked by the ➤ symbol. For example, when the procedure directs you to select **File ➤ Open**, it's telling you to click on the **File** menu and then select the **Open** command. You'll find a brief summary of basic Windows operations in the introduction to this book.

Starting Windows 95 and Excel

Your system will start Windows 95 automatically when you turn on your computer. The look of Windows 95 is different from Windows 3.1. It is also simpler to use. In Windows 95 a taskbar with a Start button appears on your screen. It is from here that you can follow the directions below to run Excel.

1 To view the Start *menu*, move the mouse pointer to the Start button on the Taskbar and click to select it.

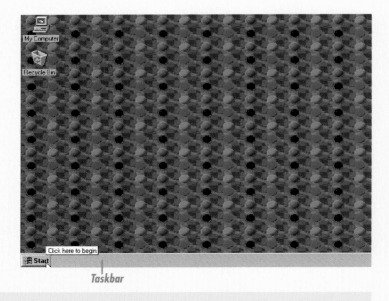

Taskbar

NOTE

If you cannot start Windows 95 by following the steps below, press the **Restart** or **Reset** button on your computer and repeat the steps. If this also fails, seek technical support.

2 On the Start menu that pops up, move the pointer to the **Programs** item. When you hold the pointer on the Programs item, a list of the programs that are installed on your machine will appear next to it. Within this Programs *folder*, move your pointer to the **Microsoft Office** item to open it.

Programs folder　　　　　　　　*Move the pointer to Microsoft Office*

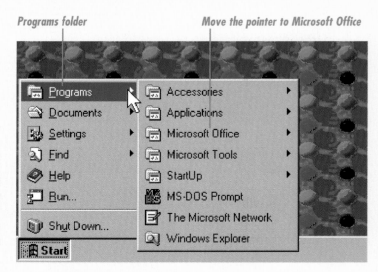

3. From the list of Office applications in this folder, select the program **Microsoft Excel** by clicking on it or moving the highlight to it and pressing ↵ (Enter) on your keyboard.

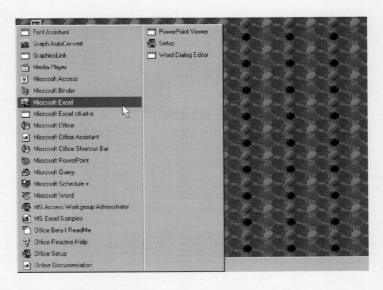

▶ The program will start and a blank worksheet will appear. The worksheet is shown in a *document window* titled Microsoft Excel Book1. The reason for this name is that the document actually contains a stack of worksheets—a *workbook*. What you are seeing in this view is the top sheet of the workbook. Along the bottom edge of the worksheet you can see the tabs for the other sheets in the workbook. You will be building your check register in Sheet1 of this workbook.

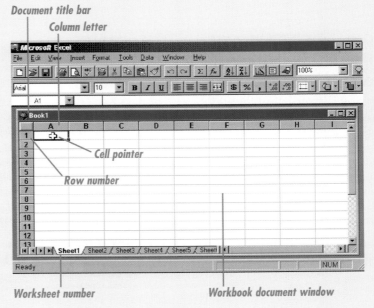

Document title bar

Column letter

Cell pointer

Row number

Worksheet number

Workbook document window

3

Exploring the Worksheet

Notice that the worksheet, or *sheet,* is composed of small rectangular areas, or *cells.* The cells are arranged in columns and rows. In the visible portion of the top sheet (Sheet1), the columns are labeled from left to right with the letters A through I. The rows are numbered from top to bottom 1 through 16. (The sheet can actually be much larger than this, but this area is a comfortable size to work with for now.)

Any cell in the sheet can be identified by the letter of its column and the number of its row, such as A1. This identifier is called a *cell reference,* or *cell address.*

The current cell, or *active cell,* is surrounded by a highlight. When just one cell is active, the highlight is an outline, as shown in the next illustration.

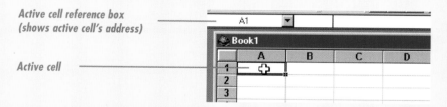

Active cell reference box
(shows active cell's address)

Active cell

When the program starts and opens Book1, the cell in the top left corner of its top sheet is highlighted. This is cell A1.

Selecting a Cell

In Excel, you must select a cell before you can enter data into it. Here's how the selection works, in one step.

1 Click a different cell within the sheet: **C4** (the cell in column C, row 4). The highlight will move as you move the *cell pointer* (a hollow plus sign) with the mouse. Note that the address (C4) of the selected, or active, cell appears in the

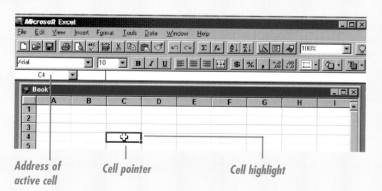

Address of
active cell

Cell pointer

Cell highlight

active cell reference box just above the worksheet window, at the top left of the screen.

Entering Data

The example in this lesson will be a check register, a record of debits and credits to a checking account. Assume that you have a stack of checks. You can begin to build the register by entering their amounts into the sheet.

1. With the highlight still in cell C4, type the amount of the first check: **15.95**. (Make sure Num Lock is on if you are using the number keys on the separate keypad.)

▶ The digits, or numeric data, you typed appeared above the sheet in the *formula bar* as you pressed the character keys. Just to the left of this text box in the formula bar is a set of four buttons,

Formula bar

5

including × and √. The ×
button means "Cancel," the
equivalent of pressing Esc
on the keyboard. The √
button means "Enter" or
"Confirm," the equivalent
of pressing ↵.

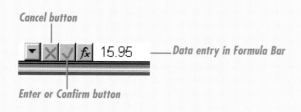

Cancel button

Data entry in Formula Bar

Enter or Confirm button

2 Press ↵. The value 15.95 is
now entered (confirmed) in
cell C4. Note that this
numeric entry is right-
aligned, or justified at the
right edge of the cell.

3 Enter the rest of the check
amounts: **64.35** in **C5**,
21.50 in **C6**, **40.00** in **C7**,
and **103.12** in **C8** (pressing
↵ or clicking on √ after
each entry).

Summing the Items

It's time to get the program to do the work by generating a total of the check amounts
you've entered.

1 Click on the cell **C10**,
which will hold the total.

2 Click on the **AutoSum** tool in the toolbar near the top center of the screen.

3 In the formula bar, click the √ button to accept the formula inserted by AutoSum.

Formula generated by AutoSum

AutoSum tool

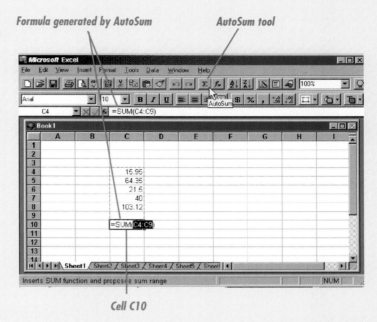

Cell C10

▶ The total will be inserted in the selected cell (C10). Column C of your sheet should now look like this:

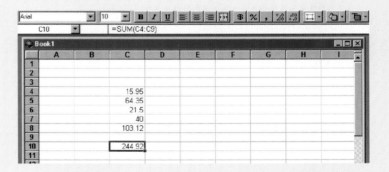

NOTE
Notice that if you move the mouse pointer to a tool, after a short time the name of the tool will pop onto the screen. With this handy feature of Excel, you need not memorize the meaning of each tool icon.

NOTE

Here's a shortcut you can use most of the time with AutoSum: If the total will be at the bottom of a column or at the right end of a row, just select the cell that will hold the total and double-click on the AutoSum tool. Double-clicking the tool in this case enters and accepts the addition formula. without your having to click on √ or press ↵.

You've Reached a Milestone!

You've now reached an important milestone in your mastery of Excel for Windows 95. You have organized data as a *range* (a column, in this case) in a worksheet. You have also used a powerful feature of the program (AutoSum) to generate a useful result.

You may be pleasantly surprised to learn that many worksheet operations are no more complex than that!

Saving Your Work

You expended some effort in generating this information. It is valuable, new work. You should store it so you can use it later.

When you are entering data into a worksheet, your entries are registered in the computer's *random access memory* (RAM). This is a kind of holding area for work in progress. However, when you turn off your computer, or even when it experiences a momentary loss of power for any reason, the contents of its memory will be lost. To save the information permanently, it is necessary to store it in a file on disk, using the following procedure.

1 Select **File ➤ Save**.

2 The Save As dialog box will appear. Notice that the program automatically assigns the file name BOOK1. However, type the new name **check**, and it will replace the name BOOK1 in the File Name text box. (The program will accept either uppercase or lowercase letters for file names.)

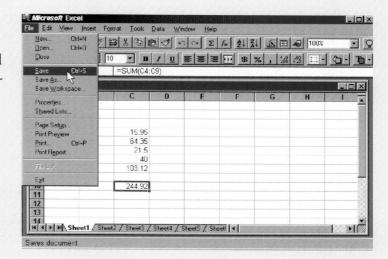

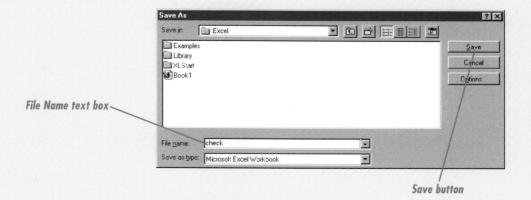

File Name text box

Save button

NOTE

In Windows 95, file names are no longer limited to eight characters with a three-character extension. Also, you can now use spaces (instead of, or in addition to, underscores) in naming your document.

3 Click on the **Save** button.

Your worksheet is now stored on disk in the workbook file CHECK, where it will remain even after your computer is turned off.

Exiting the Program

If you do not plan to start Lesson 2 right away and want to quit working in Excel, follow this step:

1 From the **File** menu, select **Exit**.

▶ The Excel application window will close, and you will be returned to the Windows 95 main interface.

In the next lesson, you will begin to concentrate more on the appearance of the check register sheet.

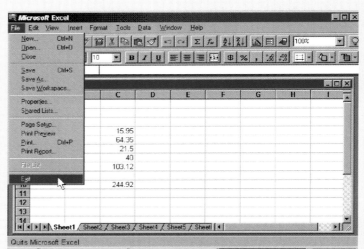

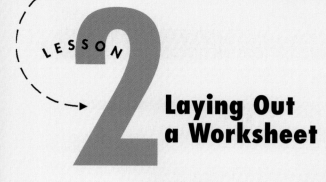

Laying Out a Worksheet

10 MINUTES

In this lesson, you will edit Sheet1 of the workbook CHECK, which you created in Lesson 1. You will add descriptive labels to the sheet. You will also rearrange the display, so that the numbers and letters of your data values and your labels align properly.

Reopening the Workbook

To begin this session, reopen the workbook by following these steps:

1 If you exited Excel at the end of the last session, restart the program by repeating the steps to open Excel (in the section "Starting Windows 95 and Excel" in Lesson 1).

2 The start-up menu bar for Excel will appear. Click on the **File** pull-down menu.

3 At the bottom of the File menu the program keeps track of the files you worked on most recently. You should see **check** listed at the bottom of the pull-down menu—click on it to reopen the file. (Or select **Open** and the Open dialog box will appear. Select the file name CHECK.)

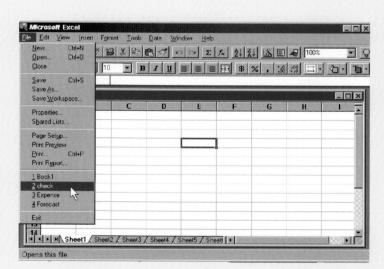

11

▶ Sheet1 of the workbook will appear in an open document window in Excel. You are ready to resume work.

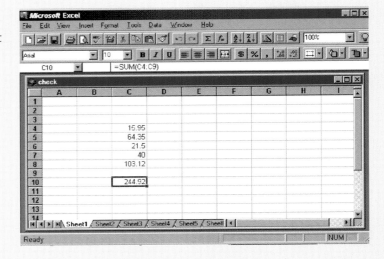

Formatting the Amounts as Currency

As you look again at the worksheet, do you notice that the program truncated some of your entries? For example, 21.50 appears as 21.5, and 40.00 appears as 40. That's because the program assumes a *style* of *Normal*, unless you specify something else. Normal style includes a *number format*—it uses no commas as thousands separators (for example, it shows 1000 instead of 1,000) and it cuts off trailing zeros from decimal values. This is not the way you are used to seeing monetary amounts, so it will be necessary to change the display.

You can change the number format of a selected cell or range by clicking one of five buttons, or *tools*, in the toolbar.

▶ As you might expect, the tool for Currency Style is labeled with a dollar sign ($).

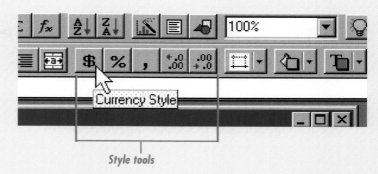

Style tools

Selecting a Range for Formatting

As a general rule, before you can make most types of changes in Excel, you must select the thing to be changed—usually the data in a cell or in a block of cells.

A block of cells is called a *range*. For example, columns and rows are two types of ranges. A range can contain multiple columns and rows, as long as the cells are contiguous (next to one another).

In Excel, the way you select a single cell is by clicking on it. But you need not work on cells one at a time. You can select an entire range by *dragging* the cell pointer from one corner of the range to another. You can select a block of cells—including several columns or rows—by starting at the top left cell of the range and dragging to the cell at the bottom right.

When you select a range, Excel highlights its cells in reverse color—white numbers against black cells, for example.

> **NOTE**
>
> Be aware that sometimes the pointer can change shape, depending on the type of mouse operation being performed. To drag the cell highlight successfully, the pointer must be shaped like a *hollow* plus sign.

See for yourself how this works as you select the check amounts and the total in preparation for changing the number formatting of all the data at the same time.

1 Click on and hold the mouse button with the pointer inside cell **C4**.

2 Keep holding the mouse button down as you move the mouse to cell **C10**.

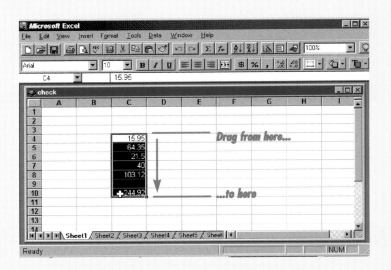

3 Release the mouse button.

Applying a Style

With the column of numbers highlighted, you can now change the style of the check amounts and the total. You will select the Currency style, which includes a leading dollar sign and two decimal places for pennies.

1 Click on the Currency Style tool ($) in the toolbar.

▶ All of the entries in the range are now displayed in Currency number format.

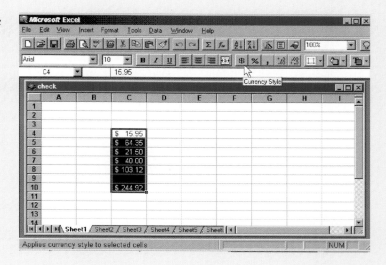

NOTE

A kind of shorthand for the range you just selected is C4:C10. The colon (:) means "and all adjacent cells including." With this notation, you can refer to a range by naming the cells at two of its corners. In this case, the range is the column of numbers from C4 through C10.

Labeling the Columns

If a worksheet were only a listing of check amounts, you could save yourself the trouble of learning how to use a spreadsheet and use a printing calculator instead. But an electronic worksheet is much more useful than that. Begin now to build something that looks a bit more like an actual check register—one that can balance itself! Start by labeling the columns.

1 Drag the pointer from **A2** to **E2** to highlight the row A2:E2.

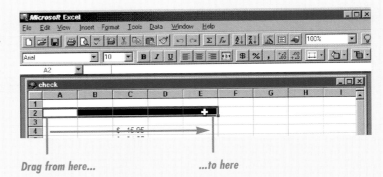

Drag from here...   *...to here*

2 Type labels as follows, pressing ↵ after each: **Date**, **Reference**, **Checks**, **Deposits**, and **Balance**.

▶ Notice how your entries flow into the selected range. In the same way, you can make your data entries flow into any block of cells *if* you drag the range first.

Centering the Labels over the Columns

Normally, the program aligns labels at the left end of their cells and aligns numbers at the right. But the check register would be more attractive if the labels were *centered* over their respective columns.

▶ The options Left Align, Center, and Right Align can be set from three buttons in the toolbar.

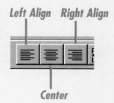

As long as the range is still highlighted, the program can change the alignment of all the labels in a single step:

1 While your entries in the row A2:E2 are still high-lighted, click on the Center tool in the toolbar.

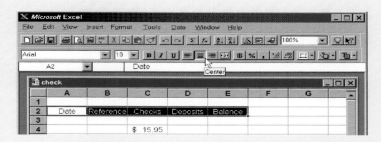

▶ The labels will be moved to the centers of their cells.

Applying Data Formats

The formatting of a cell or range can control the type of data entered into it, as well as the appearance of the data when displayed or printed out.

There are actually several ways to change the formatting of a selected cell or range. You've used the first way already—clicking on tools in the toolbar. But the choices here are somewhat limited. In the following steps, you will use two different ways to change styles and number formatting. Both work equally well. As you practice with Excel, you can use the method that seems most comfortable for you.

Changing the First Column to Date Format

The first column of the sheet you are building will hold dates of transactions. Since dates require a specific notation, it would be convenient to have Excel do the formatting automatically, just as it did for the currency amounts.

Remember that you must first highlight a cell or range before you can make menu selections or use commands that will affect it. To change the data format of a range *before* you enter date values, follow these steps:

1 Drag the pointer from cell **A4** to cell **A10** to highlight the range A4:A10.

Drag from here...

...to here

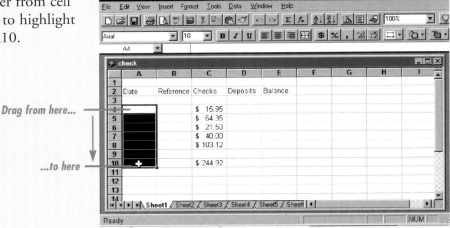

2 To see choices for number formatting, select **Format** from the menu bar, then **Cells**.

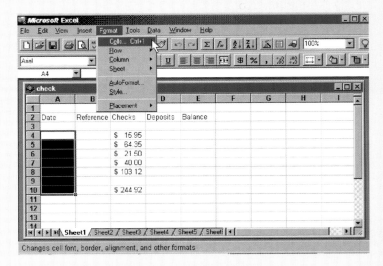

▶ The Format Cells dialog box will appear. Notice that the Format Cells dialog box has several groups of options, with each group represented as an index tab along the top edge of the dialog box. If the Number options are not currently shown, click on the tab labeled **Number** before proceeding.

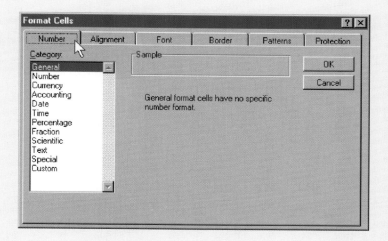

3 In the Category list, click on **Date** (the type of format). Then from the **Type** list that appears alongside the Category list, select **3/4/94**, the second entry. This is the date type we will use.

4 Click on **OK** to close the dialog box.

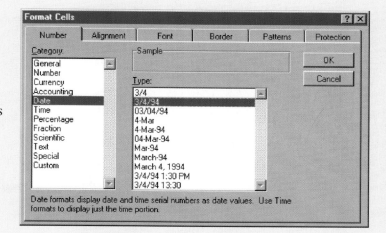

19

▶ The range of cells A4:A10 should still be highlighted. Now, regardless of how you enter dates into these cells, the display type will always have the same format as the date type we selected in the Format Cells dialog box. In the next step, you'll enter some data to see how this works.

These cells will show calendar dates in a consistent style

5 With range A4:A9 highlighted, type the following entries, pressing ↵ after each one:

    1/3/97

    1-5-1997

    01-06-97

    01/06/97

    1/6/1997

▶ Notice that, although you typed in dates in a variety of formats, the formatting you applied to the range generated a consistent format in the display.

Changing the Last Two Columns to Currency Format

The columns labeled Deposits and Balance will hold currency data and should be formatted accordingly. Although you could do this simply by selecting the range and clicking on the Currency Style tool (as you did previously in this lesson), try another method. This is a shortcut that offers convenience as well as more choices.

1 Drag the pointer from cell **D4** to cell **E10** to highlight the range D4:E10.

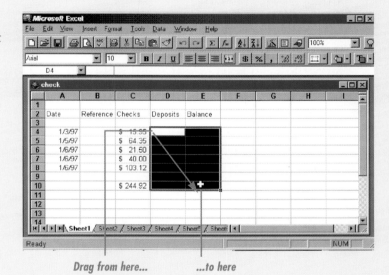

Drag from here...   *...to here*

2 Be sure that the pointer is within the selected range, and click on the *right* mouse button. A shortcut menu will pop up.

3 From the shortcut menu, select **Format Cells**.

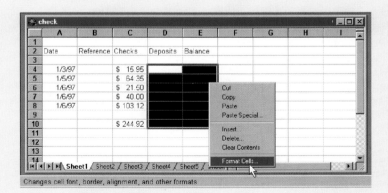

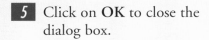 The Format Cells dialog box will appear.

4 Select **Currency** from the Category list. Then select the last entry in the Format Codes list—**$1,234.10** (Currency format with two decimal places, a comma as thousands separator, and negative values displayed in red).

5 Click on **OK** to close the dialog box.

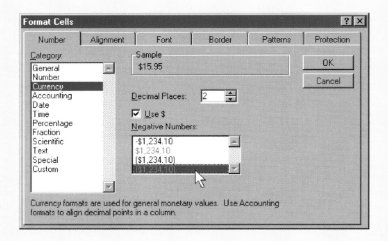

NOTE

This method of formatting is the same as selecting Format ➤ Cells, since the same dialog box appears. However, using the right mouse button as we did here to activate the selection will usually be quicker.

For now, you have nothing to enter in the Deposits column, and, since the Balance values will be calculated by the program, you can leave that column blank also.

Entering the Check Numbers

The Reference column will hold transaction numbers for checks and deposits. You don't need to apply any special formatting to this column, since the default (Normal) will work just fine. Enter the check numbers now.

1 Drag the pointer to highlight the range **B4:B8**.

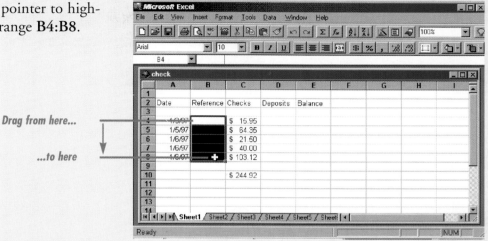

Drag from here...

...to here

2 Type these check numbers,
pressing ↵ after each entry:

721

722

723

724

725

Labeling the Last Row

Before you end this work session, add a label to the last row, which will hold the totals
of the columns that hold currency amounts.

1 Select the cell **A10**.

2 Type **Totals** and press ↵.

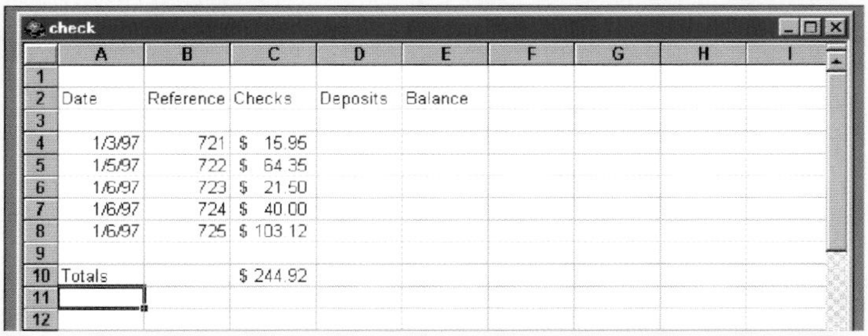

	A	B	C	D	E	F	G	H	I
1									
2	Date	Reference	Checks	Deposits	Balance				
3									
4	1/3/97	721	$ 15.95						
5	1/5/97	722	$ 64.35						
6	1/6/97	723	$ 21.50						
7	1/6/97	724	$ 40.00						
8	1/6/97	725	$ 103.12						
9									
10	Totals		$ 244.92						
11									
12									

(title bar: check)

Naming Your Sheet

You may have noticed the row of tabs along the bottom of the document screen. Normally, there are 16 tabs available to you in a workbook (although only the first six are visible). Each tab represents one sheet in a workbook. Think of the sheets as pages in a book. So, you can have as many as 16 sheets in a single workbook file.

Sixteen turns out to be a convenient number of sheets (although you can increase it if you wish). Financial records usually must be kept for each month of the 12 months of the year and for each of the four quarters. If you use one sheet for each report, that's 16 sheets in a typical workbook file.

Before you save the revised workbook, you might as well make the sheet name more meaningful than Sheet1.

1 At the bottom of the document window, double-click on the tab labeled **Sheet1**.

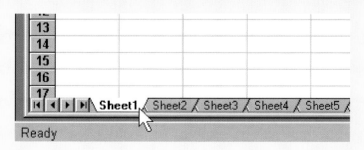

▶ The Rename Sheet dialog box will appear.

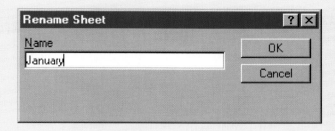

2 Type **January**.

3 Click on **OK**.

▶ The new sheet name, January, will appear on the sheet tab.

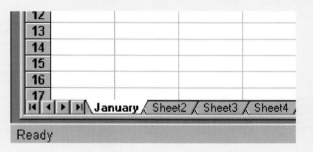

You have nearly completed the layout of the check register. In the next session, you will complete the layout. You will also add formulas, or predefined calculations, to the sheet so that it can actually generate a checkbook balance.

Saving Your Work

Always save your work at the end of a session. Since you've already named the workbook file CHECK, you don't need to use the File ➤ Save As command to assign a new name. You can save the file in a single step:

1 In the toolbar, click on the Save tool.

25

▶ The updated file will be
written to disk, replacing
the previous version of
CHECK.

2 You can now end the session and exit Excel: Select
File ➤ Exit.

3 Developing A Running Balance

30 MINUTES

In this lesson, you will edit the check register you created in Lessons 1 and 2. The completed worksheet will be able to maintain a running balance as you enter transactions for checks and deposits.

To begin this session, restart Excel and open the file named CHECK.

Providing for a Starting Balance

To begin, you must have a place to enter your starting account balance, from which your checks will be deducted and to which your deposits will be added.

Labeling the Balance Entry

To identify the cell that will hold the starting balance, add a label by following these steps:

1 Click cell **D3**.

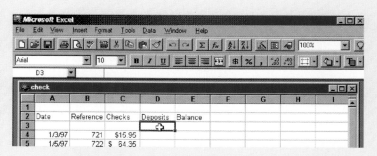

2 Type the label **Balance forward** – –>. (Use two hyphens followed by a greater-than symbol to make the arrow in your label entry in step 2. The purpose of the arrow is to provide a graphic pointer to cell E3, which will hold the starting balance amount.)

3 Instead of pressing ↵ to accept the entry, click on the Confirm button (√) in the formula bar. (This accepts the entry but leaves the position of the cell highlight unchanged.)

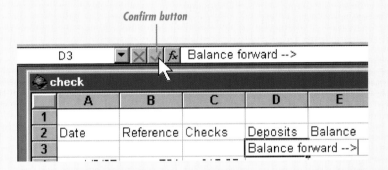

Confirm button

4 Making sure that cell D3 is still selected, click on the **Align Right** tool in the toolbar.

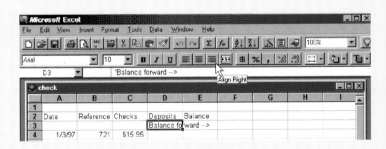

▶ The text in D3 will be realigned to the right edge of the cell.

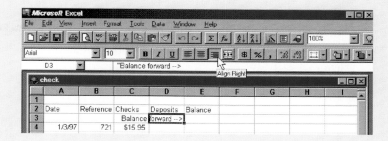

Entering a Starting Balance

Now, enter a data value for the starting balance.

1 Click on cell **E3**.

2 Type **1000**.

3 Press ↵.

▶ Cell E3 now displays a starting balance of $1,000, but the number is not formatted correctly.

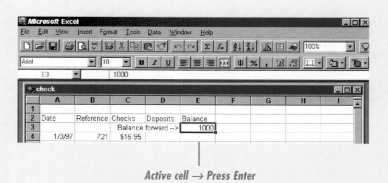

Active cell → Press Enter

As you did in Lesson 2, you could use the Format ➤ Cells command or the Currency Style tool to change the formatting. However, here's a shortcut that involves copying *just the formatting* from a cell you formatted previously.

When you pressed ↵ after entering the starting balance, the cell highlight dropped down to cell E4. Recall that you've already formatted this cell as Currency (at the conclusion of Lesson 2). With E4 already selected, here's how to quickly copy its formatting to cell E3:

1 With cell E4 selected, click on the Format Painter tool in the toolbar.

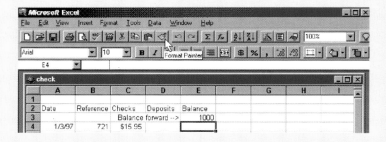

▶ The shape of the cell pointer will change to a hollow plus sign with a paintbrush, and a moving dotted line will surround the cell from which formatting is being copied:

2 Move the paintbrush-shaped pointer to cell E3 and click.

▶ The Currency number formatting has been copied from cell E4 to cell E3, but you'd never know it from the screen! Here's what you see instead.

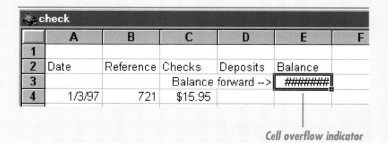

Cell overflow indicator

The cell that holds the starting balance is filled with pound signs (#). This is the *cell overflow indicator,* and it's not an error. It's just Excel's way of telling you that the cell is too narrow to show the data value stored there. You can fix this by adjusting the width of column E.

1 Move the pointer into the sheet column headings, and position it on the boundary between columns E and F (the right edge of the column you want to adjust). The pointer shape will change to a double arrow.

Double-click here

2 With the double arrow pointer on the column boundary, double-click the mouse button.

▶ Excel will adjust the column width to fit the longest entry in that column. Here's the result, including the $1,000 that seemed to be lost temporarily:

With the starting balance labeled, entered, and formatted, you're ready to add the features that will do the math of keeping the check register current.

Entering Formulas That Calculate the Running Balance

For the check register to be useful, it must maintain a running balance of the account. This can be done by way of *formulas,* or built-in calculations.

In Excel, a formula is a special type of cell entry that defines a calculation, usually in relation to other cells. Much of the power and convenience of programs like Excel comes from the ability to embed formulas in worksheets.

Actually, you already entered one formula into the sheet when you used the AutoSum tool in Lesson 1.

1 To view the formula, click on cell C10. The formula appears above the top of the sheet in the formula bar.

Formula of cell C10

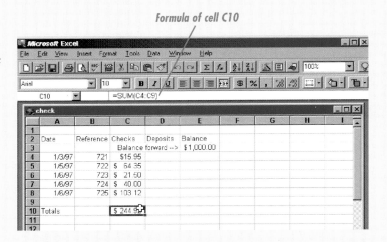

Formula Syntax (Rules of Form)

An Excel formula always begins with an equals sign (=). In the example, SUM is a *function,* or built-in type of calculation. SUM is the function for the arithmetic operation of addition.

The identifiers enclosed in parentheses show which cells will be operated on by the function. In the example, the range C4:C9 refers to all the cells in the Checks column. So, a formula that does not use the SUM function but produces the same result would be:

    =C4+C5+C6+C7+C8+C9

Entering a Formula

Enter a formula now that will calculate the checkbook balance.

1 Click on cell **E4**.

2 Type the formula **=E3–C4+D4**. (It makes no difference whether the letters are capitals or lowercase.)

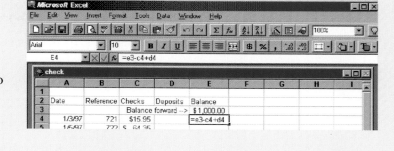

3 Click on the Confirm button (√).

▶ The formula you just entered takes the starting balance (cell E3), subtracts the check amount in C4, and adds any deposit amount in D4. The result (a data value) appears in cell E4.

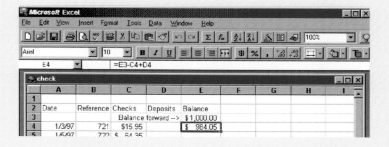

Generating More Formulas with AutoFill

You could enter a formula into each cell of column E to calculate the balance at each point. However, there's an easier way to do this.

1 With cell E4 still highlighted, move the pointer to the bottom right corner of the cell (the *fill handle*). The pointer will change to a solid plus sign.

Fill handle

2 Drag the fill handle from cell **E4** to cell **E9**, highlighting the range E4:E9.

3 Release the mouse button.

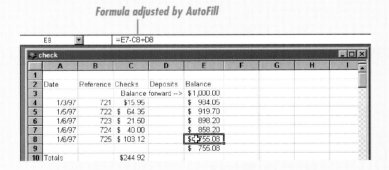

NOTE

Dragging the fill handle to copy the contents of a cell (in this case, the formula for cell E4) into adjacent cells is called the *AutoFill* feature of Excel.

When you released the mouse button after dragging the fill pointer, the formula in cell E4 was copied into each cell of the range you dragged. However, the formula wasn't simply copied. In each cell, the references in the formula were adjusted, or incremented, automatically by Excel so that the result in each case is correct.

Inspecting the AutoFill Formulas

Take a moment now to inspect the formulas that AutoFill generated.

1 Click on cell **E8**.

▶ When you select the cell, its formula is shown in the formula bar.

While you have cell E8 selected, take a closer look at the formula it contains.

=E7–C8+D8

In this formula, the cell references E3, C4, and D4 of the original formula have been adjusted automatically by the program to E7, C8, and D8. If you click on other cells in the range, you will find that the formula has been readjusted in each cell.

NOTE

When you use AutoFill to copy a formula, the program can readjust its cell references so that the results are still valid at the new locations.

Summing the Deposits

You don't yet have any entries in the Deposits column, but you will want to be able to provide for a total of deposits. You can use AutoFill again to generate this formula.

1 Click on cell **C10**.

2 While the cell is highlighted, move the cell pointer to its fill handle (bottom right corner). The pointer will change to a solid plus sign.

3 Drag the + pointer one cell to the right until the high-light includes both cells **C10** and **D10**.

4 Release the mouse button.

	A	B	C	D	E	F	G	H	I
1									
2	Date	Reference	Checks	Deposits	Balance				
3				Balance forward -->	$1,000.00				
4	1/3/97	721	$15.95		$ 984.05				
5	1/5/97	722	$ 64.35		$ 919.70				
6	1/6/97	723	$ 21.50		$ 898.20				
7	1/6/97	724	$ 40.00		$ 858.20				
8	1/6/97	725	$ 103.12		$ 755.08				
9					$ 755.08				
10	Totals		$ 244.92	$ -					
11									

Drag from here...   *...to here*

Now, if you click on cell D10, you will see its contents above the sheet in the
formula bar:

=SUM(D4:D9)

This is precisely the formula you need to generate the Deposits total, and the program
derived it from the Checks total formula in C10, just as expected. (The program treats
the blank cells in the Deposits column as zeroes.)

Entering a Formula for the Current Balance

The current checkbook balance will be shown in column E on the line of the last
transaction entered. However, to assure the accuracy of this electronic check register, it
would be a good idea to provide another way of developing the balance. In accounting
terms, this is similar to the practice of *cross-footing* a manual spreadsheet. That is, the
sum of the columns should equal the sum of the rows: You should be able to get the
same grand total by adding either down or across the sheet.

In the case of the check register, you should be able to calculate the balance by sub-
tracting the total in the Checks column (cell C10) from the starting balance in E3 and
adding any deposits (D10). A formula for this calculation would be

=E3–C10+D10

Enter this formula into the sheet now.

1 Click on cell **E10**.

2 Type the formula
=E3–C10+D10.

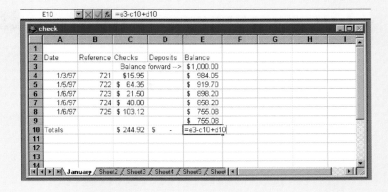

3 Press ↵.

▶ The result of the formula
will appear in cell E10.

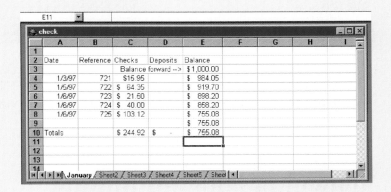

Putting the Worksheet to Work!

By now, you've provided for all the formulas required to calculate the check register.
Any new transaction, whether check or deposit, that you enter will cause the whole
sheet to be recalculated automatically. That is, each time you make a data entry in the
check register, the program will update the totals and balance.

See this for yourself. Enter a deposit item of $250 on 1/6/95, and let Excel do the rest.

1 Click on cell **D6**.

2 Type the deposit amount:
250.

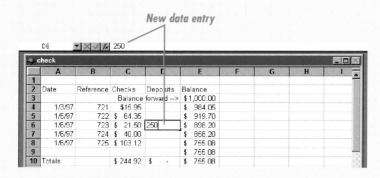

New data entry

3 Press ↵.

▶ The check register will be
recalculated to allow for the
newly entered deposit.

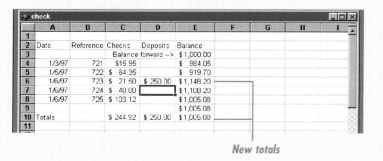

New totals

Expanding the Sheet

Although it is now functional, this check register lacks a feature that would make it
truly convenient: It should be possible for the check listing to grow (as you add more
items and rows) so that an ongoing register can be maintained.

One of the difficulties in expanding the sheet lies in the way it has been designed. The
Totals row limits addition of check listings. One solution is to put the Totals row on
top of the sheet.

Moving a Row Using Drag-and-Drop

Move the Totals row now using the *drag-and-drop* method.

1 Click and drag to highlight the row **A10:E10** (the bottom row of totals), then release the mouse button.

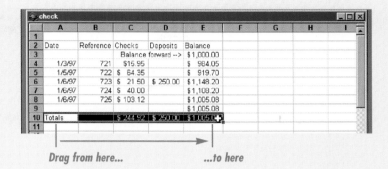

Drag from here...   ...to here

2 Move the pointer to any edge of the highlighted range until its shape changes to an arrow.

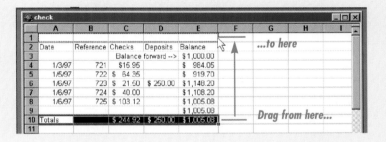

3 Click and hold the mouse button. Keep holding the button down as you drag the row up into the row **A1:E1**. (An outline of the range will move with the pointer.)

4 Release the mouse button.

▶ The range you selected and dragged has been moved to the location A1:E1.

Formatting the Rest of the Sheet

Notice that row 9 has no data entries but includes the Balance formula. It is always good practice to leave a blank, formatted row in this manner, so that you can copy it to expand the sheet when necessary.

1 Making sure the pointer is within cell **A9**, click and drag to highlight the row **A9:E9**, then release the mouse button.

2 Move the cell pointer to the fill handle (bottom right corner of cell E9). The pointer shape will change to a solid plus sign.

3 Drag the + pointer downward and *off the bottom of the sheet*, as you continue to hold down the mouse button. The display will begin to scroll.

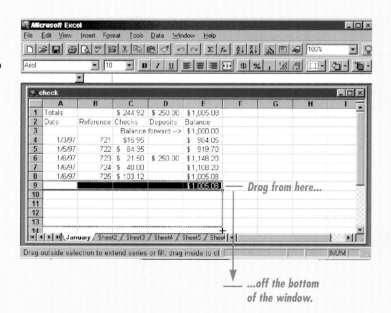

Drag from here...

...off the bottom of the window.

4 Keep holding down the button as the rows scroll past. Release the mouse button at row 100.

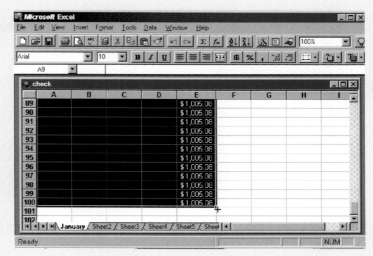

▶ AutoFill copies the formulas from the blank row into the rows you have just highlighted.

If you run out of room for the month of January, you can always repeat this procedure. (In February, you should start a new sheet.)

NOTE
To make it easy to expand the sheet later, be sure to leave one blank row that can be used for copying.

Going to the Top of the Sheet

The cell pointer should now be at cell E100. In preparation for the next series of steps:

1 Press **Ctrl+Home**. (While holding down the Ctrl key, press the Home key.)

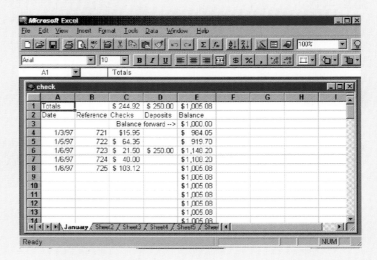

▶ The Totals row—the top of the sheet—should now be displayed.

Editing the Formulas

Even though the program readjusted the formulas when you moved the Totals row, the formulas that generate the Checks and Deposits totals don't now include all the new cells in the sheet. You must edit the formulas to include the new cells.

1   *Double-click* on cell **C1**.

▶ The formula for the total of the Checks column appears in the cell and in the formula bar.

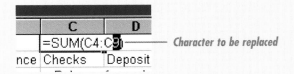

2   In either the formula bar or in cell C1, drag the I-beam cursor over the digit 9 to highlight it.

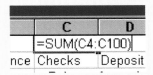

Character to be replaced

3   Type the replacement value: **100**.

4   Click on √ to enter the formula.

▶ The edited formula is entered into the cell, and its result appears there.

Revised formula

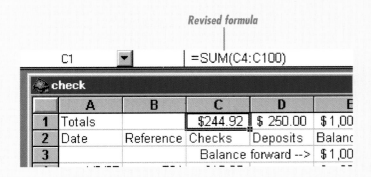

5 Select cell **D1** and repeat steps 1 through 4 to change its formula to read:

=SUM(D4:D100)

6 Click on √ to enter the formula.

▶ Again, the edited formula is entered into the cell, and its result appears there.

| D1 | ▼ | | =SUM(D4:D100) |

check

	A	B	C	D	E
1	Totals		$244.92	$ 250.00	$1,00
2	Date	Reference	Checks	Deposits	Baland
3			Balance forward -->	$1,00	

> **NOTE**
>
> Double-clicking on the cell opens its contents for editing. As in a word processing applica-tion, the *insertion point* appears as a flashing vertical bar. When you move the cell pointer into the open cell, its shape changes to an *I-beam cursor*. You can change the position of the insertion point by moving the insertion point within the cell and clicking. Or, you can drag the I-beam over a group of characters that you want to replace. You can make your edit in the cell or in the formula bar: The I-beam cursor works the same way in each location.

Splitting the Window

The check register now includes enough rows for 97 transaction items (100 rows minus the first 3). However, as the listing grows, it will become inconvenient to keep scrolling between the bottom and the top. Excel has a handy solution for this.

1 Click on cell **A4**.

2 From the **Window** pull-down menu, select **Split**.

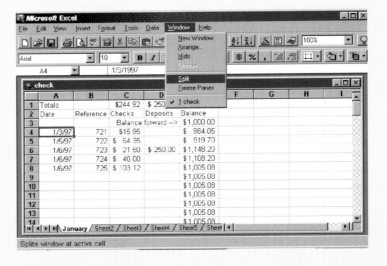

▶ Two separate views of the same sheet are opened, split just above the selected cell (A4, in this case).

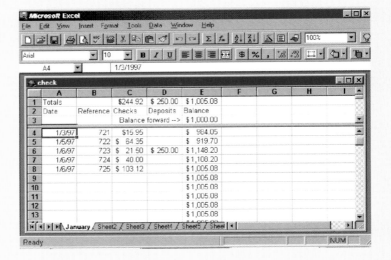

Adjusting the Views

You can move the cell pointer and adjust the scroll boxes separately to adjust the view in each window. To use the check register, adjust the scroll box in the vertical scroll bar in the lower window to advance to new transaction-entry rows. As you do this, the first three rows of the sheet (including Totals) will remain stationary on top.

To scroll the display, you can do either of the following:

- Drag the button in the scroll bar to move through large portions of the sheet.

- *Or* click on the arrow buttons to adjust the display one row at a time.

Try this now:

1 In the lower half of the split, click on the bottom arrow button once.

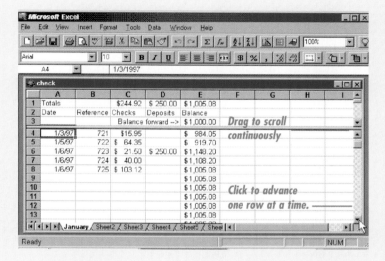

▶ The display will be advanced down the sheet by one row.

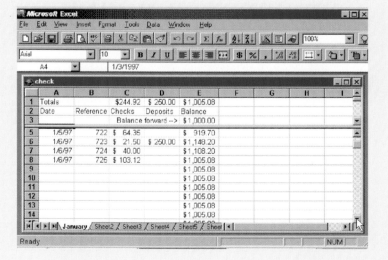

NOTE

You can remove the split whenever the sheet is open by selecting **Window ➤ Remove Split**.

Using the Check Register

You now have a fully workable check register!

Remember to leave a blank row at the bottom so that you can expand the sheet quickly and easily to hold more transactions. If you expand the sheet, adjust the formulas that generate totals of checks and deposits. Notice that the repeating totals in column E indicate the extent of unused, but valid, rows. If you come to a row that shows no balance, it contains no formulas and *cannot hold valid entries*. Expand the sheet and readjust the formulas before you enter more transactions.

When you have filled the sheet with one month's transactions, it will be time to open another copy of the sheet to begin the next month. You'll learn how to create a *template* for this purpose in Lesson 5.

Saving Your Work

Conclude this session—and preserve the check register for your ongoing use—by saving CHECK to disk.

NOTE

If you save a workbook when the sheet is split, the split view will appear when you reopen the file. The cell pointer will be located just where it was when the file was saved, ready for you to resume work!

You can save the current workbook by clicking on the Save tool, as described in Lesson 1. However, here's the command method, which can be selected with either the mouse or the keyboard and may be easier to remember:

1 From the menu bar, select **File ➤ Save**.

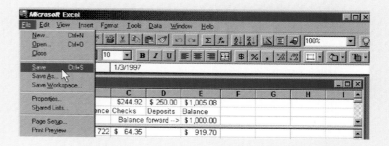

2 If you won't be doing Lesson 4 right away, select **File ➤ Exit** to quit Excel. Otherwise, continue on to the next lesson.

In the next lesson, you will begin to build another sheet—your monthly expense report. You will then use this sheet in several lessons that cover appearance formatting, printing, sorting expense items by account number, and worksheet outlining.

4 Designing an Expense Report

5 MINUTES

In this lesson, you will use the skills you picked up in the first part of this book to create a new worksheet, an employee expense report. You will find that the steps to set up the sheet and its formulas are similar to the ones you took to create the check register. However, this time you will also discover some new techniques that can help make it quick and easy for you to do even more ambitious projects.

To begin this lesson:

1 Start Excel (if you need help, refer to Lesson 1).

▶ You'll see the empty document window named Book1.

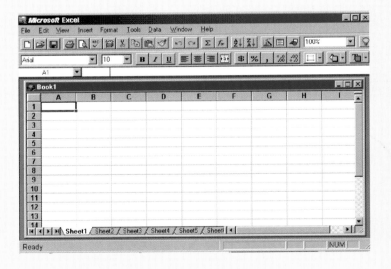

Entering a Title, Text, and Column Headings

Start to lay out the sheet by entering some descriptive text labels. When you begin a new workbook, notice that the cell highlight appears in cell A1.

1 Type the sheet title **Monthly Expense Report** and press ↵. The cell highlight will drop down to cell A2.

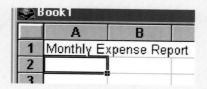

2 Type **Name:** and press ↵.

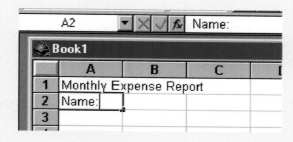

3 Click on cell **D2**.

4 Type **Department:** and press ↵.

5 Click on cell **G2**.

6 Type **Date:** and press ↵.

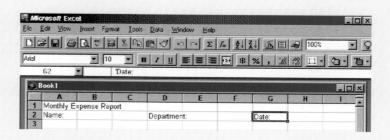

▶ You now need to select the row A3:H3 in preparation for entering the column headings. (If you select the range first, your data entries will flow into it, eliminating the need to select each cell individually.)

7 Click and drag to highlight the range **A3:H3**. (Click and hold on A3, keep holding the mouse button down as you move the pointer to H3, then release the mouse button.)

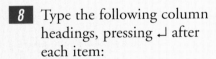

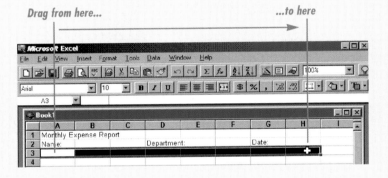

8 Type the following column headings, pressing ↵ after each item:

        Date

        Description

        Transportation

        Lodging

        Meals

        Misc

        Totals

        Account

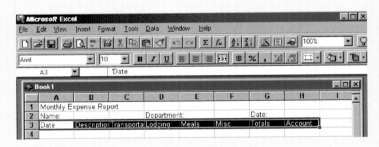

Adjusting Alignment of Labels and Column Width

Note that the labels Department, Description, and Transportation are too long for the cells that contain them (D2, B3, and C3). Fix the layout of the labels and columns now by first choosing Center alignment for all the labels, then adjusting the column widths. (You'll use the same procedure for adjusting column width that was covered in Lesson 3.)

1 With A3:H3 still selected, click on the **Center** tool to center all the headings in the row over the columns.

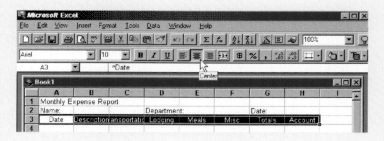

2 Move the pointer into the sheet column headings, and position it on the boundary between columns **B** and **C**. The pointer shape will change to a double arrow.

3 With the pointer on the boundary of columns B and C, double-click the mouse button.

▶ Column B widens to fit the longest entry (in this case, the label Description).

4 Follow the same procedure (steps 2 and 3) to adjust the widths of columns **C and D**.

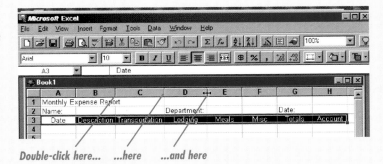

Double-click here...   ...here   ...and here

NOTE

You have other options for adjusting column width and row height. Rather than double-clicking on the border as just described, you can *drag* the double-arrow pointer instead. This permits you to adjust the column or row to any width or height you want. Or, to make these adjustments instead by numeric values (text point size), you can use the menu commands Format ➤ Column ➤ Width and Format ➤ Row ➤ Height.

Adding the Remaining Text Labels

There are just three more text labels required for this sheet. Enter them now.

1 Click on cell **A14**.

2 Type **Totals** and press ↵.

3 Click on cell **F15**.

4 Type **Less advances** and press ↵.

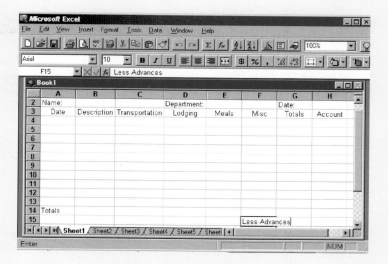

5 Type **Amount owed you** and press ↵.

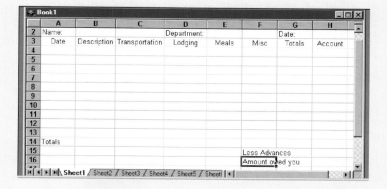

6 Click and drag to highlight the range **F15:F16** (two cells containing labels).

7 Click on the **Align Right** tool.

▶ The labels in F15 and F16 will now be right-aligned with the values that will appear in cells G15 and G16.

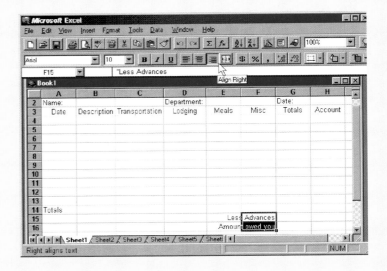

Applying Data Formats

You have completed the basic layout of the expense report form. To provide for accurate displays, apply data formats now to the columns that will hold dates and currency amounts.

Applying Date Format

1 Click and drag to highlight the range A4:A13.

2 Click the right mouse button to activate a shortcut menu.

3 From the menu, select **Format Cells**.

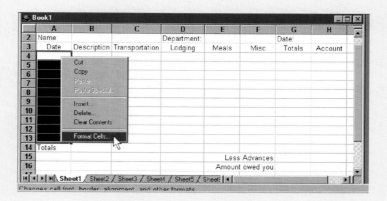

▶ The Format Cells dialog box will open.

4 If the Number page of options is not displayed, click on the **Number** tab at the top of the dialog box.

5 In the Category list box, select **Date**.

6 The format code *3/4/94* is suitable, so simply select it and click on **OK** to accept the entries and close the dialog box.

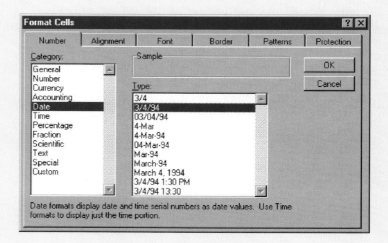

55

Applying Currency Format

Now, apply the Currency format to the cells that will contain monetary amounts.

1 Click and drag to highlight the range **C4:G14**.

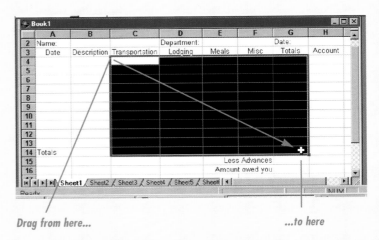

Drag from here...   *...to here*

▶ In fact, you will need cells G15 and G16 to be formatted the same way as the range you have selected—to display amounts as currency. To show you how you can add cells to a selection, do the following step now.

2 While holding down **Ctrl**, click on cells **G15** and **G16**. These cells will be added to your range selection.

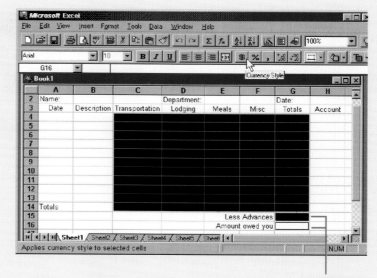

Ctrl-click to add these cells to the selection

3 Click on the **Currency Style** tool ($) in the toolbar.

Aligning the Accounts Column

The Account column (H) will hold general-ledger account numbers to which expense items must be charged. The report will be more attractive if the entries in this column are aligned right instead of left (left alignment is the default). Change the alignment now.

1 Click and drag to highlight the range **H4:H15**.

2 Click on the **Align Right** tool in the toolbar.

The sheet isn't quite finished yet, but here's an opportunity to do some computer "housekeeping."

Saving Your Work So Far

Although you haven't finished this lesson yet, you have done a significant amount of work: You've entered all the labels and number-formatted the data ranges. It's good practice to save your work not only at the conclusion of each lesson but also at such intermediate points to prevent losing data due to accidents, such as disruptions of electrical power.

1 Save the workbook file as **EXPENSE**. (As explained in previous lessons, click on the Save tool or select File ➤ Save from the menu.)

NOTE

When you save a new file, the option Save File As Type in the Save As dialog box must be set to Microsoft Excel Workbook, the default. Once you've saved a workbook file, the Save As dialog box will not reappear the next time you save the file by using the Save tool or the File ➤ Save command; the file will simply be saved under the existing name. To rename a file upon saving it, select File ➤ Save As instead.

Defining Range Names

Recall that a notation with two cell addresses linked by a colon specifies a worksheet *range*. This is the method used to specify ranges in the formulas you included in the check register. However, specifying ranges by explicit addresses can become tedious, especially as you begin to build and edit larger sheets. Furthermore, the addresses in a range reference are simply locations and tell you nothing about the range itself. It would be convenient to have a more meaningful way of specifying ranges.

An alternative method of specifying ranges is to give them *names*, much as you would name a variable in an algebra problem. You can then insert the name of a range in formulas rather than insert the explicit addresses. This is usually more convenient and—perhaps more important—makes the formulas in your sheet more understandable. This way, if you must revise a sheet you haven't used in a while, you will have little difficulty understanding its formulas at a glance.

Now, name some of the ranges in the Expense sheet in preparation for entering formulas.

1 Click and drag to highlight the range **C4:C13** (the Transportation column).

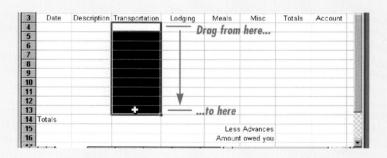

2 In the formula bar, click on the **Name** drop-down arrow, which appears just to the right of the Names box/cell address box.

3 Type **transport** and press ↵.

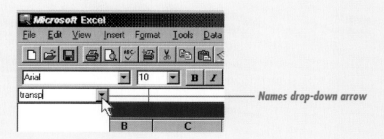

4 Repeat steps 1 through 3 for each of the following ranges and names: **D4:D13** (**lodging**), **E4:E13** (**meals**), and **F4:F13** (**misc**).

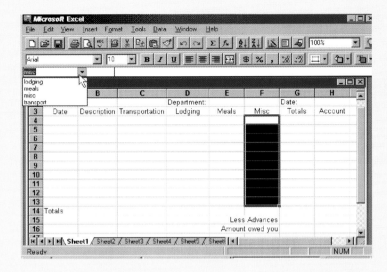

▶ A range can also be a single cell, so individual cells also can have range names. This will come in handy for two other cells in the sheet:

5 Using the procedure just described, give cell **G14** the range name **total** and give cell **G15** the name **advances**.

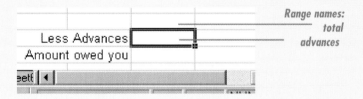

Range names:
total
advances

6 You can now inspect all of the range names in the sheet by clicking on the Names drop-down arrow.

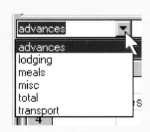

Excel's naming feature gives you at least two benefits:

● When you open the Names drop-down box, you can select all the cells in a range simply by clicking on the range's name.

● In formulas, you can refer to the range names rather than using explicit cell addresses.

In Lessons 1 and 2, you used AutoSum and AutoFill to generate formulas for arithmetic totals. Now that you have named each of the columns of expense categories in this sheet, you have an alternative way of developing the totals. Follow these steps to see how you can use range names in formulas:

1 Select cell **C14**.

2 Type =**sum(**

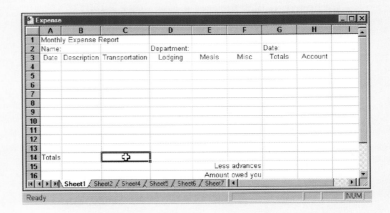

3 Click on the **Names** drop-down arrow.

4 Click on the **transport** range name.

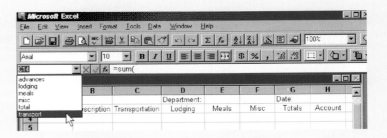

5 Click on the √ button in
the formula bar.

When you click on √, Excel adds the closing parenthesis to the formula and capitalizes
the function name, indicating that it is valid. The program then enters the formula
into the selected cell (C14) and calculates the result (0 in this case, since the blanks in
the column are treated as zeros). You could have typed this formula into the formula
bar, but the procedure just described has an advantage beyond its convenience: when
you select an existing range name to insert into a formula, you will never misspell it!

Recall that an Excel formula always begins with an equals sign (=). In cell C14, you
entered a formula that contains the SUM function, which is a built-in formula for the
arithmetic operation of addition. This time, instead of *cell addresses*, the identifier
enclosed in parentheses is the *range name*.

The program simply substitutes the corresponding cell addresses each time it encoun-
ters a range name. For example, using the **transport** range name in this formula is the
same as entering

    =SUM(C4:C13)

And using the SUM function is the same as entering each cell in the following
calculation:

    =C4+C5+C6+C7+C8+C9+C10+C11+C12+C13

Another advantage of using a range name is that you need not keep track of addresses
if you move the range or otherwise edit the sheet. The program will adjust the cell
addresses as necessary, and the range name will be unchanged.

Entering Formulas for the Other Expense Categories

Now use the range names you've already defined in formulas for the totals of the other
expense categories.

1 Use the procedure just
described to enter formulas
as follows:

Cell	Formula
D14	=SUM(lodging)
E14	=SUM(meals)
F14	=SUM(misc)

▶ When you've entered the
formulas for each category
total, the sheet should look
like the illustration.

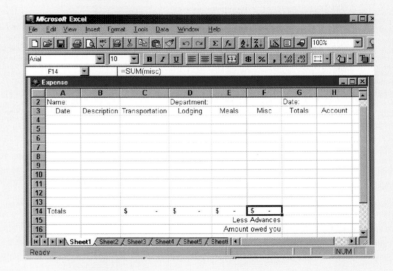

Providing for the Row Totals

You want to sum the entries across the form, by row, as well as down the form, by column. On an expense report, the row totals typically represent daily expenditures in all
categories. In the following steps, you will use the AutoSum tool to generate the basic
formula, then use AutoFill to apply the formula to all the rows in the sheet.

1 Click on cell **G4**.

2 Click on the **AutoSum** tool *once*.

3 Drag the pointer from **C4** to **F4** so that the dotted-line reference box includes the range C4:F4.

4 Release the mouse button.

5 Click on √.

▶ The AutoSum tool generates the following formula and inserts it in the selected cell (G4):

=SUM(C4:F4)

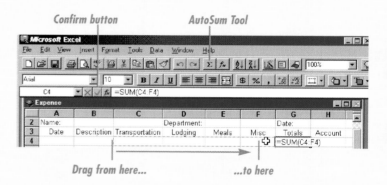

Confirm button   *AutoSum Tool*

Drag from here...   *...to here*

Recall from Lesson 3 that you can use the AutoFill feature to copy this formula to adjacent ranges in the sheet. Do this now to copy the formula into the rest of the cells in the Totals column.

1 With cell G4 still selected, move the pointer to the fill handle (the small square in the bottom-right corner of the highlighted cell border). The pointer shape will change to a solid plus sign.

2 Drag the fill handle from cell **G4** to cell **G14**.

3 Release the mouse button.

▶ The program will adjust the cell addresses so that they refer to the correct row in each instance.

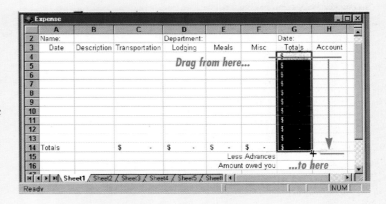

Calculating the Reimbursement Amount

You have one more formula, which will calculate the amount of your reimbursement to enter into this sheet. Since you have already assigned names to the ranges required, you can insert them in the formula.

1 Select cell **G16**.

2 Type **=total–advances**.

3 Click on √ (or press ↵).

▶ The sheet should look like this.

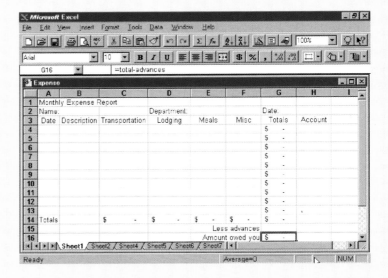

NOTE

Rather than typing the range names in the formula, you can select them from the Names drop-down box, as you've already done in this lesson. But if you should type the names and make a mistake, don't worry. Excel will catch the error. Instead of a numeric result, the error value **#NAME?** will appear in the cell. To correct the formula, double-click on the cell and edit the misspelled range name.

The formula **total–advances** performs arithmetic subtraction. The minus sign indicates that the amount in cell G15 will be subtracted from the amount in cell G14. The result is your net cash outlay, or the amount you spent that exceeded the cash advances you received. This is also the amount you want paid back to you, so the adjusted total is labeled Amount Owed You. It will be displayed in cell G16 (the cell that contains the formula).

Saving the Completed
Worksheet Layout

You have completed all the steps required to create a fully functional worksheet that will report expenses and calculate the amount owed you.

Before ending this lesson, be sure to save your work. You can use the Save tool or the File ➤ Save command as already described, or you can try the following *shortcut key* combinations:

- Hold down **Ctrl** and press **S**. The updated sheet will be saved to the existing workbook file EXPENSE.

- You can exit Excel by using another shortcut key combination: Hold down **Alt** while you press **F4** twice. The first time you press Alt+F4 you close the worksheet. The second time you press Alt+F4 you exit Excel.

> **NOTE**
> Shortcut keys are available as convenient alternatives for some of the more commonly used commands. If an Excel shortcut key is available, it will be shown opposite the command in its pull-down menu. (The **Alt-F4** shortcut key, however, is a feature of Windows, and is not shown on the File pull-down menu in Excel.)

In the next lesson you will enter data into the sheet and work on its appearance.

LESSON

5 Formatting the Expense Report

5 MINUTES

In Lesson 4, you designed an employee expense report, including laying out the sheet and embedding calculations as formulas. When you designed the sheet, you applied number formats to certain columns to cause them to be displayed properly as dates or as currency amounts.

In this lesson, you will learn about some other types of formatting, which affect the appearance of the worksheet. You will also learn how to use the expense form as a *template,* or model, for generating monthly expense reports.

Opening the Expense File

Once you have restarted Windows and the Excel application, begin this lesson by reopening the EXPENSE document file you saved at the conclusion of Lesson 4. As an alternative to selecting File ➤ Open, try another method, which uses a feature of the toolbar. (Begin by starting Excel, if the program is not already running.)

1 From the toolbar, select the **Open** tool, the second one from the left.

▶ The Open dialog box will appear, with worksheet files in the current folder listed under the File Name box.

2 In the file listing, select the file name **Expense.**

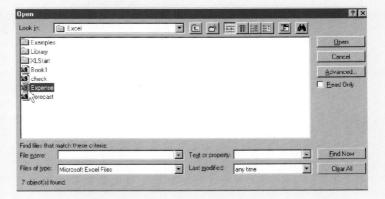

▶ The workbook file will be loaded into an Excel document window.

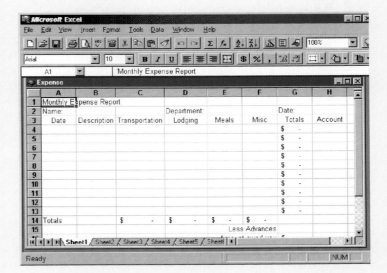

NOTE

The instructions here assume that you saved the workbook file under the default folder EXCEL. If you saved the file to another location, you must type the path and file name in the File Name box or navigate the Folders and Drives boxes to log on to the correct folder before you select the file name.

Using AutoFormat

Excel has a feature called AutoFormat that allows you to apply predesigned appearance formats to your own worksheets. Try it now. You must first select the range within the sheet that will be formatted. Instead of dragging the range, take the following steps to select it. (You may find this selection method convenient for large blocks of cells.)

1 Click on cell **A3**.

2 While holding down **Shift**, click in cell **H14**. (This procedure selects a block of cells as though you had dragged to select the range A3:H14.)

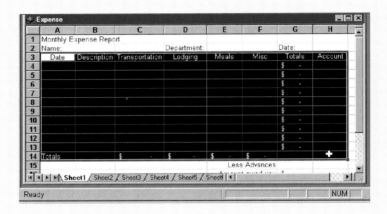

3 With the range highlighted, select **Format ➤ AutoFormat**.

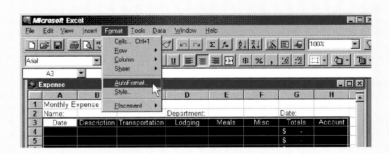

▶ The AutoFormat dialog box will appear. In the AutoFormat dialog box, names of predesigned formats are listed in the Table Format box on the left, and a view of the current selection (Simple) is displayed in the Sample box on the right.

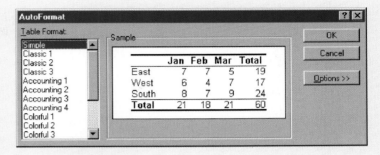

Selecting a Ready-Made Format

With a single command, the AutoFormat feature of Excel applies a well-designed assortment of appearance formats to your selection. With the AutoFormat dialog box still open, try it now.

1 In the Table Format list box, click on the ↓ button and scroll down the list until the selection *List 1* appears.

2 Click on **List 1**. A view of your selection will appear in the Sample box.

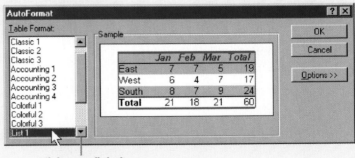

Click to scroll the list

3 Select **OK** to accept the entry and close the dialog box. (If you do not need to see the Sample display, you can simply double-click on your selection.)

▶ The Expense sheet will appear in the document window, and its appearance will be changed to match the List 1 format. Note that colors are shown in reverse because the selected range is still highlighted. (To de-select the range and view it in its true colors, you can make another selection in the sheet.)

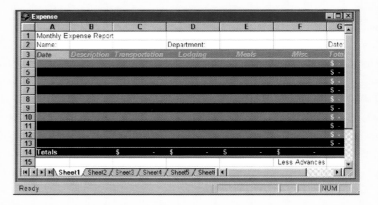

4 In preparation for the next step, drag the row **A1:H1**, which includes the sheet title Monthly Expense Report and spans all the columns. (In doing this, you will need to drag the cell pointer off the right side of the window. The display will scroll. Release the mouse button at cell H1.)

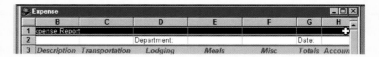

Formatting the Report Title

You'd expect the title of the report to be bigger and bolder, perhaps in a different font, and centered across the form, so you'll do that next.

Centering a Label across Columns

You can fix the centering first, in a single step.

1 With the row A1:H1 still highlighted, click on the **Center Across Columns** tool.

Changing Fonts

Although this step is optional, you might try changing the font of the report title. Changing fonts in Excel works much the same way it does in other Windows applications.

The title should still be highlighted. Although you've selected the entire row A1:H1 and centered the title within it, the text is actually still stored in its original location—cell A1.

1 With the title still selected, click on the ↓ button to the right of the **Font** drop-down box in the toolbar.

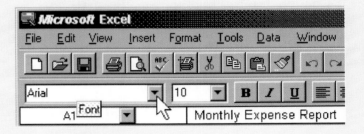

▶ A list of fonts installed for the current printer in Windows will open.

2 Adjust the scroll bar to see more font names: Scroll the list until you see *Times New Roman*.

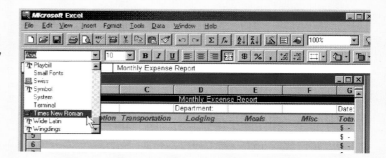

3 Click on the font name **Times New Roman**, which both selects it and closes the Font drop-down box.

Changing Font Attributes

Now, increase the text size (the height of the characters measured in *points*) and add the Bold and Italic attributes to the title:

1 In the toolbar, click on the ↓ button to the right of the **Font Size** box to open it.

▶ A list of numeric text sizes (in points) will appear.

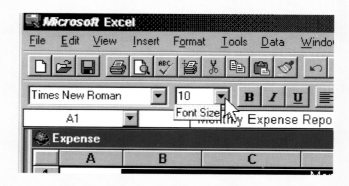

2 Click on **18** to select the size, which also closes the drop-down box.

3 Click on the **Bold** tool (also in the toolbar).

4 Click on the **Italic** tool.

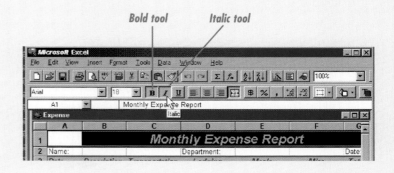

Bold tool   *Italic tool*

Changing Text Color

Unless you have a color printer, the colors you select in Excel will only affect the display on the screen. To change the color of the report title, follow these steps:

1 With the title still selected, click on the ↓ button on the **Font Color** drop-down box. A palette of colors will appear.

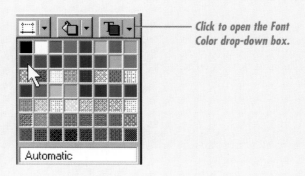

Click to open the Font Color drop-down box.

2 In the palette, click on a color, such as **Dark Red**, which also closes this drop-down box.

Maximizing the Document Window

To work with the other labels in the report, it will be convenient to make the document window as large as possible on the screen.

1 Click on the **Maximize** button in the top right corner of the EXPENSE workbook document window.

▶ The current sheet will be enlarged to fill the screen, and the Maximize button changes to a **Restore** button.

Document window's Restore button

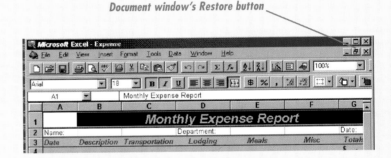

Working with Appearance Formats

Although the program has done much of the appearance formatting, this sheet has some extra items that need individual attention. For one thing, the appearance would be improved further if all the labels matched.

You might be tempted to use the Format Painter tool, which was introduced in Lesson 3, to copy the existing text formatting to the other labels. However, when you use this tool, *all* of the formatting goes along for the ride—including not only font and font attributes, but also cell background color, border, and text alignment. So, in this case, that approach won't be convenient.

You could change the font attributes of the labels as you just did for the report title—that is, select each cell individually and change the Bold, Italic, and Color attributes. However, as an introduction to a wider variety of formatting options, follow the steps below instead, to change the appearance formatting of all the other labels at the same time.

Changing Options for a Multiple Selection

You can select multiple cells or ranges—even if they are not adjacent to one another—then perform a single set of appearance changes. Try this now with the remaining labels in the sheet.

1 Click on cell **A2**.

2 While holding down **Ctrl**, click on the following cells to be added to your selection: **D2**, **G2**, **A14**, **F15**, and **F16**.

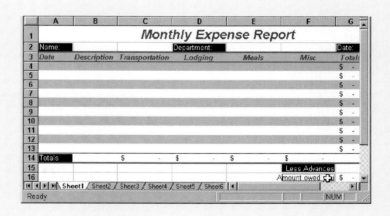

3 Click the right mouse button. A shortcut menu will appear.

4 Select **Format Cells**.

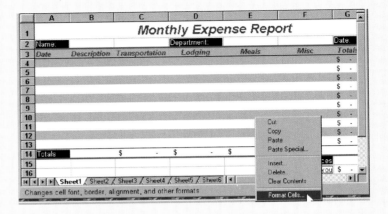

▶ The Format Cells dialog box will appear. (You have already worked with the Number options in this dialog box, in Lessons 2 and 4.)

5 Among the row of tabs at the top of this dialog box, click on **Font**.

▶ Options for fonts and font attributes will appear.

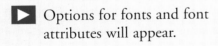
Set these two options

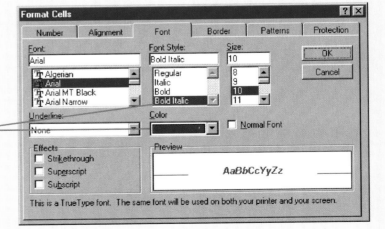

6 Within this dialog box, click on **Bold Italic** in the Font Style box.

7 Still in this dialog box, click on the ↓ button to the right of the Color drop-down box to open it, adjust the scroll bar if necessary, then click on the same **Dark Red** color you selected for the title earlier in this lesson. (A scroll bar will appear if you have a display that can show 256 or more colors.)

8 Click on **OK** to close the Format Cells dialog box.

9 Click on any other cell in the sheet to release the current selection.

▶ You will see that the font options for all the labels now match the previously formatted column headings.

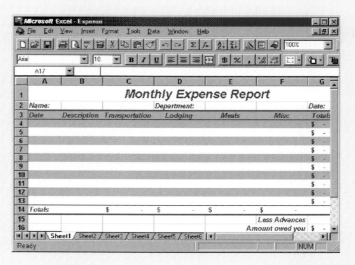

Adding Borders and Shading

The List 1 table format you applied with the AutoFormat feature includes not only font settings but some other appearance options as well. The ruled lines are types of cell *borders,* and the gray bands are a *shading* option.

Selecting a Cell Border

Create a border now that will highlight the Amount Owed You on your report.

1 Click and drag to highlight the range **E16:G16**.

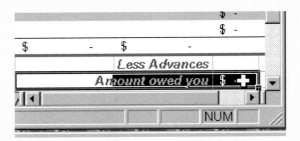

2 In the toolbar, click on the ↓ button on the right of the **Borders** tool. An assortment of borders will appear for you to choose from.

3 In the Borders drop-down box, click on the bottom-right representation, the one indicating a bold border on all four sides of the cells you've highlighted.

Borders drop-down arrow

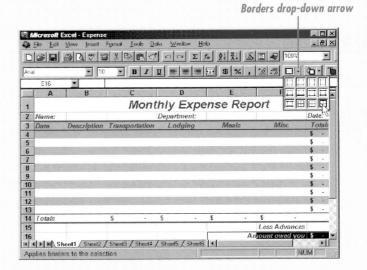

Selecting Shading to Fill the Cells

Now, use another feature in the toolbar to change the color of the filled area within the cells you've already highlighted.

1 With E16:G16 still highlighted, click on the ↓ button on the **Color** tool in the toolbar.

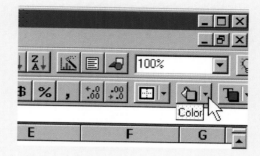

2 In the Color drop-down box, click on the **Light Gray** color patch (second row, second color from the right).

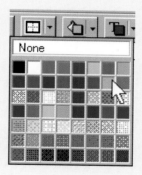

3 Click on any cell *outside* the current selection (E16:G16) to remove the highlight and view the new border and shading.

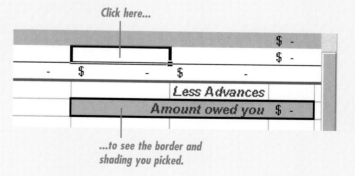

Click here...

...to see the border and shading you picked.

Saving the Sheet

You have completed the employee expense report, which is fully functional and self-calculating, as well as attractive in appearance. Save it now (in a single step) to prevent losing all this productive work.

1 In the toolbar, click on the **Save** tool.

Using the Worksheet

It's time to put the sheet to work for you.

Entering Data

In the following steps, you will enter sample data, as well as learn a technique for clearing, or erasing, data from the sheet.

1 Click and drag to select the row **A4:F4**.

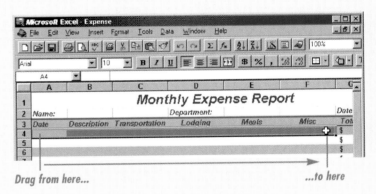

Drag from here...   ...to here

2 Type the following data items, pressing ↵ after each entry:

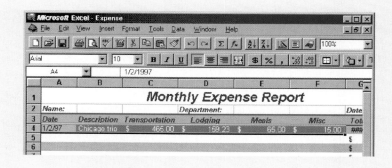

    1-2-97

    Chicago trip

    465

    159.23

    65

    15

▶ The data will appear in the selected range, and the sheet will calculate all required totals. Note how the program formats the date and currency values automatically. For now, ignore the cell overflow indicators (#####) in column G.

Continue to enter data into the next row, and watch what happens.

3 Click and drag to select the row **A5:F5**.

4 Type the following data items, pressing ↵ after each entry:

> 1-7-97
>
> Wisconsin trip
>
> 1293.45
>
> 487.91
>
> 589.56
>
> 26

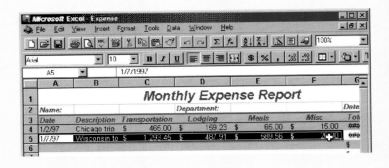

Adjusting Column Width

Notice the value display in some of the cells. The display shows ##### instead of some of the values. Recall from Lesson 3 that this is not an error. These *cell overflow indicators* tell you that the Totals column is not wide enough to hold the calculated values. (The width of the cells is shown by the number of pound signs (#), one for each available character position.) Fix the column width now.

1 Move the pointer to the right edge of the **G** column heading, so that the pointer changes to a double arrow.

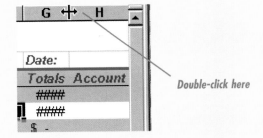

Double-click here

2 Double-click the mouse button.

▶ The width of column G is adjusted automatically to fit its longest entry.

Notice also that the some of the text in column B (Description entries) appears to be cut off on the right side. This is what happens when *text* entries are too long for the column width. Fix that now, but use a different technique that lets you decide just how wide the column should be.

1 Move the pointer to the right edge of the **B** column heading so that the pointer changes to a double arrow.

2 Drag the pointer to the right.

3 Release the mouse button when the column is a bit wider than the "Wisconsin trip" entry, leaving room for some longer entries.

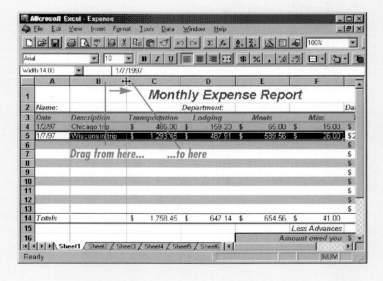

4 Save the latest version of the sheet to disk by clicking on the **Save** tool.

NOTE

Because the sheet is now wider than the document window, you must adjust the scroll bar at the bottom of the screen to see columns G and H. Don't be concerned with column H for now. You will use this column in subsequent lessons to hold account classifications for your expenses.

Clearing Data Values

The data you have entered in this lesson is now held on disk along with the sheet format, in the workbook file EXPENSE. If you want to reuse this sheet to create another report, you first must clear the data values, leaving the formatting intact. Excel provides a convenient way to do this.

NOTE

When you are selecting ranges in which data will be cleared, be sure *not* to include cells that contain formulas (the totals, in this case). For purposes of clearing, formulas are treated like data values and will be erased. As long as a formula is valid, there is no need to clear it, since the value displayed at its location depends entirely on data entries in *other* cells.

1 To select all data values in the sheet, click and drag to highlight the range **A4:F5**.

2 Move the pointer to the fill handle (lower right corner) of the selected range. The pointer will change to a solid plus sign.

3 Drag the pointer (fill handle) upward to the top edge of the range, then release the mouse button.

▶ Only the data values will be cleared, leaving the formatting intact so that you can make new entries in the sheet.

Drag the fill handle from here... ...to here

Making Copies of the Sheet

Remember from Lesson 2 that a typical workbook can have as many as 16 sheets. For your expense reports, it would be convenient to keep reports for the current year in a single workbook file, with a separate sheet for each month.

Here's how to make copies of your blank, formatted expense report that will be included in the template you're about to create.

1 From the menu bar, select **Edit ➤ Move Or Copy Sheet**.

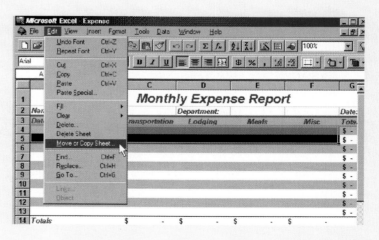

2 The Move Or Copy dialog
box will open. Mark the
check box **Create A Copy**.

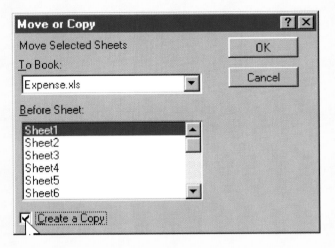

3 Click on **OK** to close the
dialog box.

▶ A copy of Sheet1 will be
inserted into the work-
book. The tab at the bot-
tom of the copy will be
labeled **Sheet1 (2)**.

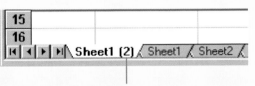

(Optionally, double-click to rename the sheet)

NOTE

You can repeat the Edit ➤ Move Or Copy Sheet command to insert more copies of the
blank sheet into the workbook. As demonstrated in Lesson 1, you can double-click on the
sheet's tab to give it a more meaningful name (such as *January*). At this point, you need
only two copies of the formatted sheet in your template file. As long as you always have
one blank, formatted sheet in a workbook, you can repeat the Edit ➤ Move Or Copy
command to copy this sheet each time you start a new report for the current month.

Saving the Workbook as a Template

As a further convenience, you can save your stack of blank, formatted sheets as a *template,* or model, for other workbooks. Once you save the template to the folder named **Templates,** Excel will present the template **Expense** in the list of selections whenever you select File ➤ New. This way, you can create a series of reports without affecting the template you use as a master.

Save the expense report workbook now as a template file.

1 Select **File ➤ Save As**.

▶ The Save As dialog box will appear.

2 In the dialog box, open the Save As Type drop-down list box.

3 From the drop-down list, select **Template**.

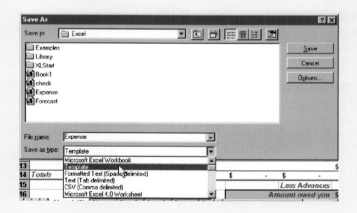

▶ The program will automatically place the template in the Templates folder.

4 Click on **Save** to close the dialog box.

5 Close the workbook file: Select **File ➤ Close**. (You have already saved the sheet in its latest version, along with the first two rows of expense data.)

Applying a Template

Before you end this lesson, you can demonstrate to yourself how using a template can make quick and easy work of doing repetitive reports.

1 From the menu bar, select **File ➤ New**.

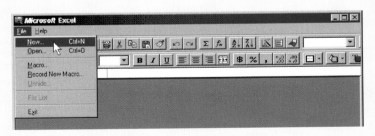

2 The New dialog box will appear. In its list of template names, double-click on **Expense**.

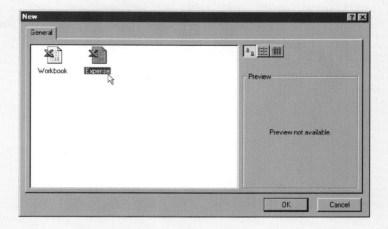

▶ A new workbook document will be opened, formatted according to this template. Note that the program has assigned the name **Expense1**, which appears in the title bar of the document window.

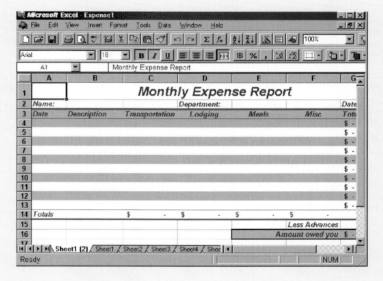

You can now enter data into this new workbook. When you save it, the file name will be **EXPENSE1**. The next time you create a new workbook from the template, the name **Expense2** will be assigned. That is, the program will keep track of the workbook file names so that they follow one another in sequential order, based on the name of the template from which they were created.

NOTE
To open the template itself for editing, select its name in the New dialog box, then hold down **Shift** as you click on **OK**. This opens the template (.xlt file) rather than creating a new document (.xls file) based on the template.

In the next lesson, you will preview and print the expense report.

6 Previewing and Printing the Expense Report

10 MINUTES

In this lesson, you will preview the expense report sheet on the screen so that you can make final adjustments to its appearance. Then you will print it out as a completed report.

Setting Up Your Printer in Windows

Excel will print only to the default printer, which you must have selected previously in the Windows Control Panel. Before continuing this lesson, take the following steps to be sure that your printer is set up properly.

1 If you have the Excel application open, click on its **Minimize** button.

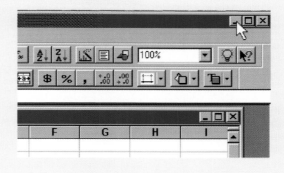

▶ The Excel application will remain minimized on the Taskbar until you restore it with a mouse click.

2 In the Windows 95 main interface, click on the **Start** button.

3 In the Start menu, click on **Settings**. The Settings menu will open.

4 In the Settings menu, click on **Printers**.

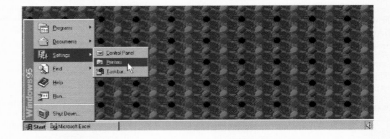

▶ The Printers dialog box will open, showing either a list of the printers available to you or a group of icons representing them. To set a default printer, follow steps 5 and 6.

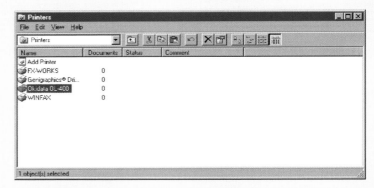

5 In the Printers dialog box, click on the printer you want to use (for example, **Okidata OL-400**).

6 From the **File** menu select **Set As Default**, if it is not already checked.

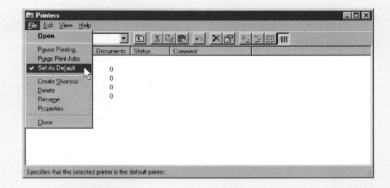

7 Select **Close** to close the Printers dialog box.

NOTE

This procedure selects the default printer for use by all Windows applications. To install a printer not shown in the Printers dialog box, select **Add Printer**, which brings up the Add Printer Wizard. Follow its prompts for installing new printers. If you wish to use a printer other than the system default, you can select File ➤ Print ➤ Printer from the Excel menu bar. Your selection here will apply only to Excel work sessions, overriding the system default printer setting.

Opening the Expense Sheet

Having set up your printer, follow these steps to reopen the sheet you saved at the end of Lesson 5:

1 Restart Excel. (If you minimized it previously, simply
click on it on the Taskbar.)

2 In the toolbar, click on the
Open button.

▶ The Open dialog box will
appear.

3 In the File Name listing,
double-click on **Expense**.

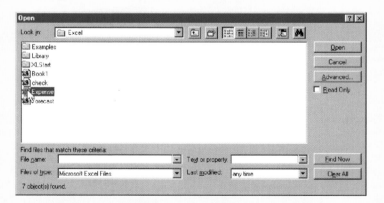

4 The document window for this workbook file will open. If the window is not already maximized from the previous lesson, click on its **Maximize** button.

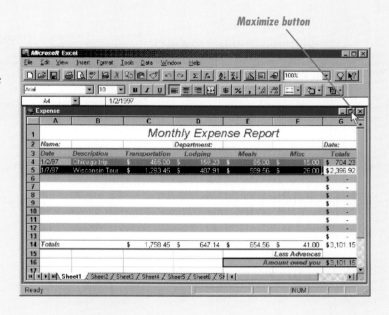

Maximize button

Making Final Data Entries

To complete the expense report, you will need to enter a few more data items: your name, your department, the date, and the amount of any cash advances.

1 Click on cell **B2**.

2 Type your name and press ↵.

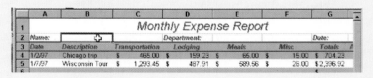

3 Click on cell **E2**.

4 Type **Marketing** and press ↵.

5 Click on the → button in the bottom scroll bar to move the display horizontally by columns so that column H is visible.

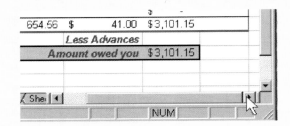

6 Click on cell **H2**.

7 Type **1/3/97** and press ↵.

8 Click on cell **G15**.

9 Type **500** and press ↵.

▶ When you enter the amount of your cash advances in cell G15, cell G16, which uses that value in the formula **=total–advances**, will be updated.

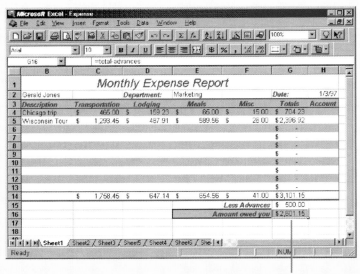

The cell automatically updates.

98

Previewing the Printed Report

Excel has a way for you to inspect the appearance of the printed document before you produce the actual output. You can also make final adjustments to the appearance of the document at this point.

1 Click on the **Print Preview** tool in the toolbar. (Clicking on this tool is equivalent to selecting File ➤ Print Preview from the menu bar.)

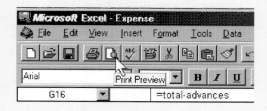

▶ A full-screen preview of the sheet will appear.

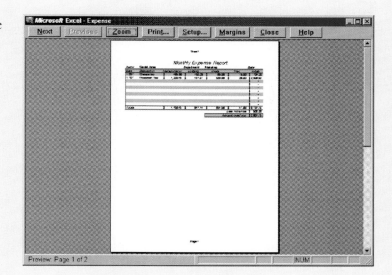

Changing to Landscape Orientation

In the preceding illustration, the page is set up initially for portrait orientation, which has the long dimension of the paper running vertically. This is the default printer setting you would want to use if you also do a fair amount of word processing on your computer. However, landscape orientation (in which the long dimension is horizontal) is usually preferred for printing worksheets. In this case, switching to landscape will also prevent the last column being cut off, making it possible to print the report on a single page. You can change this setting within Excel.

1 In the row of buttons at the top of the preview screen, click on **Setup**.

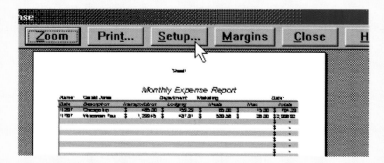

2 The Page Setup dialog box will appear. If the Page options aren't displayed, click on the **Page** tab.

3 Within the Page sheet of options, click on the **Landscape** option button.

4 Be sure that the paper size shown is correct. If not, make your selection in the **Paper Size** drop-down list box.

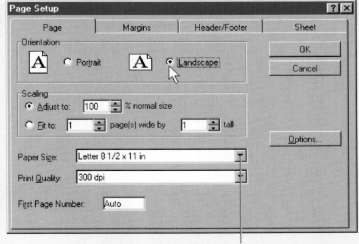

Click to change Paper Size if necessary

5 Select **OK** to close the dialog box.

▶ All of the columns of the report will now be displayed, starting in the top left corner of a landscape page.

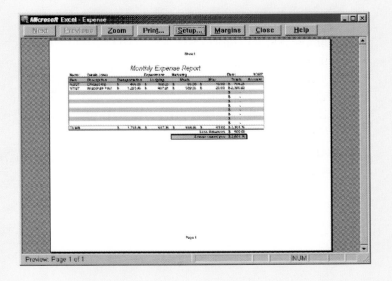

Adjusting the Margins

Although the appearance of the printout has been improved, it's still not quite right. The report is not centered on the page. Fix that now.

1 In the row of buttons at the top of the preview screen, click on **Margins**.

▶ Handles, shown as small black squares, will appear around the edges of the previewed page.

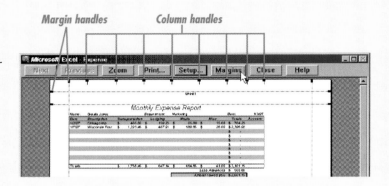

The handles at the corners are margins, and the others are column borders. You can adjust any of these—thereby changing the sheet display—simply by dragging the handle.

However—when your report can fit easily within the borders of a page, there's an even quicker and easier way to make sure that it is centered. Try it now.

1 Still in Preview mode, click on the **Setup** button.

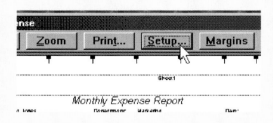

2 The Page Setup dialog box will appear. Click on its **Margins** index tab. The page's Margins options will appear in the dialog box.

3 Mark both of the Center On Page check boxes: **Horizontally** and **Vertically**.

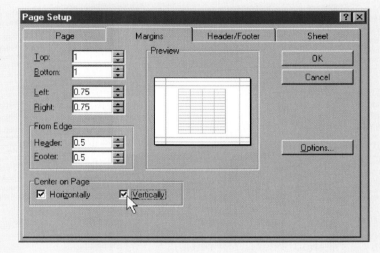

4 Click on **OK** to close the dialog box.

▶ Your report will reappear in Preview mode, this time centered on the page.

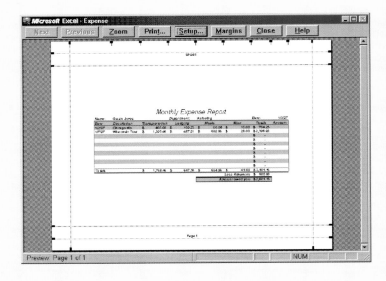

Zooming the View

The numbers in your report look rather small in Preview mode. (By default, data values are displayed in 10-point Arial type.) There's a fast way to inspect them up close without having to print the report first.

1 Move the pointer into the cell with the value for "Amount owed you" at the bottom right of the worksheet. The pointer will change to a magnifying glass.

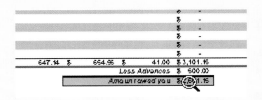

2 While the pointer is still shaped like a magnifying glass and positioned over the data value, click the mouse button.

▶ A zoomed (enlarged) view of the sheet will appear.

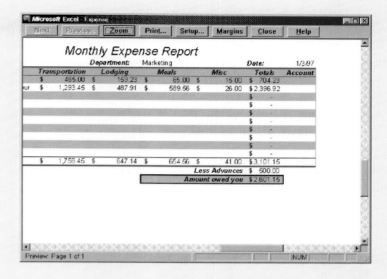

Printing the Sheet

You are now finished with your adjustments to the previewed version of the sheet and can print the document. Be sure that your printer is switched on and that its On-Line indicator is lit, then follow these steps:

1 In the row of buttons at the top of the preview screen, click on **Print**.

2 The Print dialog box will appear. If you want multiple copies of the document, click on the ↑ button on the right side of the Copies text box to increase the number of copies (to **2**, for example).

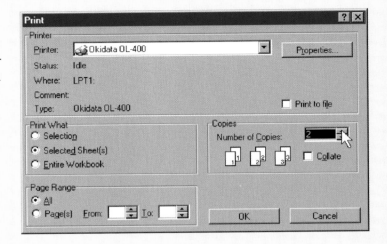

3 Click on **OK** to close the dialog box and start printing.

The sheet will print out, and the program display will return to the workbook document window. When you receive the printout, notice that the program added the name of the sheet at the top of the page and a page number at the bottom.

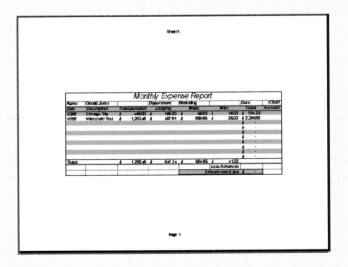

Using the Print Tool

Setup options, such as printer orientation and page margins, are saved with the Excel workbook file, so you only need to set them once, unless you want to change the layout. Once these settings are made, you can print the sheet in a single step.

1 On the Standard Toolbar, click on the **Print** tool.

▶ The prompts and dialog boxes offering setup options will be bypassed, and the document will be printed immediately.

Printing a Portion of a Sheet

Suppose you want to print only a portion of a sheet. If the setup options have already been selected, you can also do this with the Print tool.

1 In the Expense sheet, select the range **A3:G5**. (If the sheet has been scrolled so that A3 isn't shown, you can drag from G5 leftward to A3. The display will scroll as you drag.)

2 From the menu bar, select **File ➤ Print**. The Print dialog box will appear.

107

3 Among the Print What options, click on the **Selection** option button.

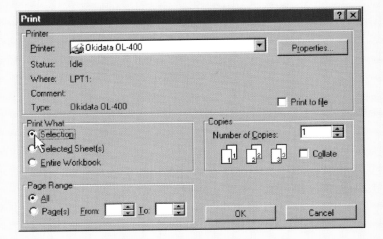

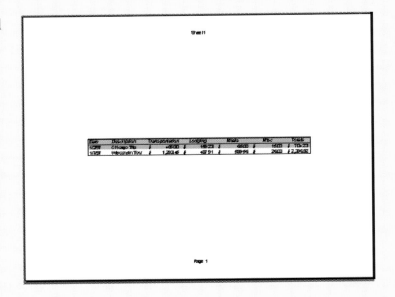

Only the selected range will be printed, with the addition of the sheet name at the top and the page number at the bottom.

If you need to quit Excel before going on to the next lesson, select **File ➤ Exit**. Select **Yes** in response to the prompt *Save Changes to Expense?*

Sorting Expenses by Account

15 MINUTES

In this lesson, you will apply a feature of Excel that is quick, easy to use, and very powerful—the Data ➤ Sort command. The purpose of sorting the data—reordering the entries according to specified criteria—will be to prepare a breakdown of subtotals for each account, or expense category.

Until now, the Account column of your expense report has been blank. This space is provided for the entry of account numbers, to which line items will be charged. The account numbers typically would be taken from your company's chart of accounts, or master list of categories for income and expense items.

In the following steps, you will enter more expense data, assign account numbers to each line of the report, and then sort the data by account number.

Starting Excel and Opening the Sheet

Begin this lesson by starting Excel and opening the Expense sheet. This time, try an alternative way of retrieving the file instead of using the Open tool. (Restart Excel if you have left it.)

1 From Excel's menu bar, select **File**.

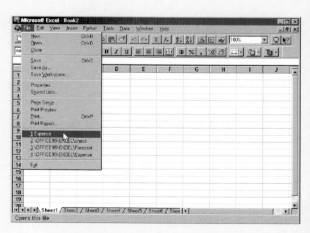

2 If the Expense workbook is among the last four files you worked on, its file name will be listed near the bottom of the pull-down menu. If so, select **EXPENSE**. If not, open the file using the method you used at the beginning of Lesson 5.

Entering Expense Data

After you select the file, its document window will open. Now, enter some more expense items into the sheet.

1 Drag the row **A6:F6**. (If the display is scrolled so far that you can't see A6, you can drag from F6 leftward to A6, then press **Tab** to make A6 the first cell to receive data.)

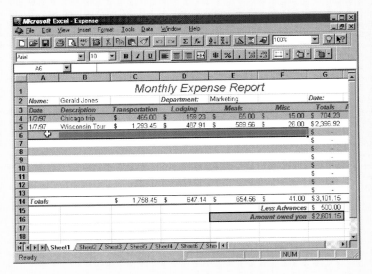

2 Type the following data entries, pressing ↵ after each one (where it says <blank>, make no entry and just press ↵):

    1-10-97
    Lunch - Apex
    <blank>
    <blank>
    54
    5

▶ Your data entries will flow into the highlighted row.

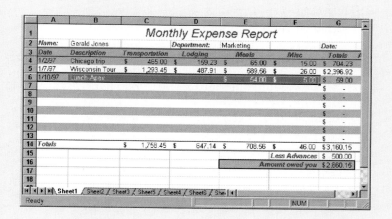

3 Click and drag to highlight (select) the range **A7:F7**.

4 Type these entries, pressing ↵ after each one: **1-13-97, Dinner - Marcom**, <blank>, <blank>, **184, 12.**

5 Select the range **A8:F8**.

6 Enter **1-16-97, SIA conference, 325, 56, 23.50, 3**.

7 Select the range **A9:F9**.

8 Enter **1-17-97, Lunch - XCorp**, <blank>, <blank>, **43, 2**.

9 Select the range **A10:F10**.

10 Enter **1-23-97, Lunch - Apex**, <blank>, <blank>, **76, 5**.

11 Select the range **A11:F11**.

12 Enter **1-24-97, Supplies**, <blank>, <blank>, <blank>, **13.93**.

13 Select the range **A12:F12**.

14 Enter **1-27-97, Ohio tour, 1496.54, 236, 154, 15**.

15 Select the range **A13:C13**.

16 Enter **1-30-97, Car allowance, 345**.

▶ The report now shows all of your expenses for January.

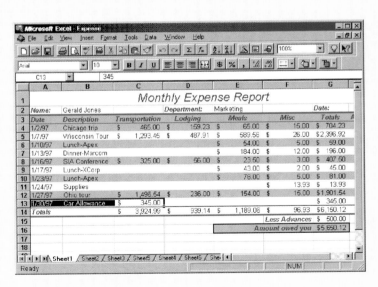

Entering the Account Numbers

You can now assign each of the line items on the report to a specific numbered account. Assume that your company's chart of accounts includes the following categories:

Account Number	Account Name
803	Car expense
811	Office expense
816	Travel expense
817	Meals and entertainment

Each of these account numbers, in turn, can have subaccounts, or more specific categories. In the expense report example, there might be a separate subaccount for each client company. For example, Apex Chemicals might be subaccount 17. The account number for meals and entertainment charged to this subaccount, then, would be

817.17

Enter account numbers now for each of the line items in the report.

1 Scroll the display to show column H (Account): Click on the → button in the horizontal scroll bar twice to move the display over two columns.

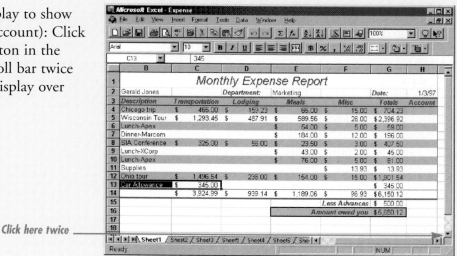

Click here twice

2 Click on cell **H4**.

3 Type the following entries,
pressing ↵ after each one:
**816.12, 816.15, 817.17,
817.11, 816.14, 817.18,
817.17, 811, 816.13, 803.**

▶ Your entries fill column H,
and you have provided an
account category for each
line of your report.

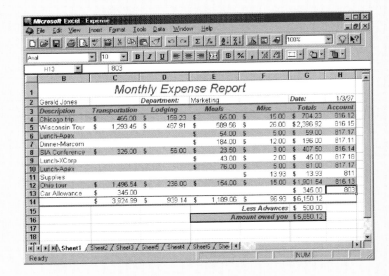

Building a Table

Having entered the account numbers, you should now create a table to hold the sorted
account totals.

Selecting the Sort Range

First, you must select the data that will be sorted. This can be done in a single step.

1 Click and drag the range **G4:H13** (the two columns containing expense totals and the corresponding account numbers).

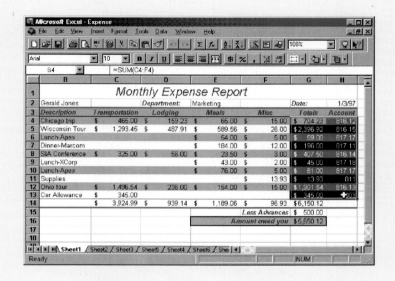

It would destroy the chronological order of the report to sort these items in place, or within the report itself. Instead, you should create a separate table.

Copying and Pasting Data Values

To create the table of account totals, you need to copy the selected range to another part of the sheet. However, you don't want to copy the formulas, just the data values. You can do this with the Edit ➤ Paste Special command.

1 With the range G4:H13 still highlighted, click the right mouse button. A shortcut menu will appear.

2 From the shortcut menu, select **Copy**.

3 Click on the ↓ button in the vertical scroll bar ten times, until row 27 is shown at the bottom of the window.

4 Click on the ← button in the horizontal scroll bar twice until column A is shown in the window.

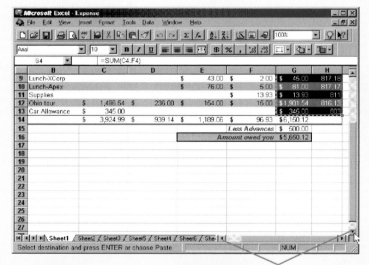

Click these buttons to scroll the display.

5 Click on cell **B17**. (You need only select the first, or top left, cell of a range into which data will be pasted.)

6 Click the right mouse button. A shortcut menu will appear.

7 From the shortcut menu, select **Paste Special**.

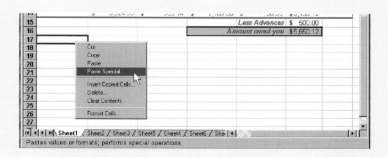

8 The Paste Special dialog box will appear. Among its Paste options, select the **Values** option button.

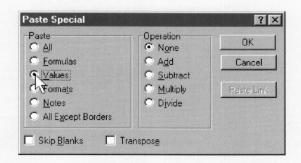

9 Click on **OK** to close the dialog box.

▶ The values you copied—including the results rather than the formulas in the selected range—will be pasted into the sheet, starting at cell B17. (Notice that the Currency data formatting was *not* copied. You can fix that later.)

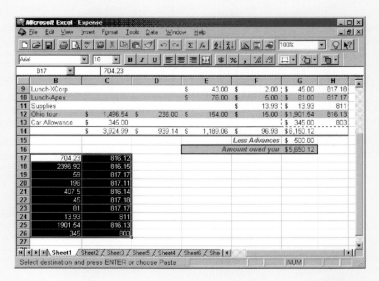

Moving a Range

As it now stands, you have a two-column table: The expense totals are on the right, the account numbers on the left. But it would be more convenient if the columns were transposed—with the account numbers on the left, the expense totals on the right. You can rearrange the table now by moving the data in column C to column A.

1 Select the range **C17:C26**.

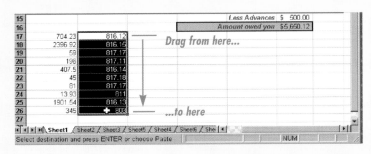

2 Move the cell pointer to any edge of your selection until the pointer shape changes to an arrowhead.

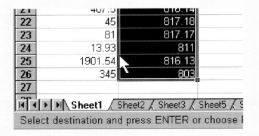

3 Making sure that the pointer is still an arrowhead, hold down the mouse button and drag the data left-ward—from column C to column A.

4 Release the mouse button.

Drag from here...
...to here

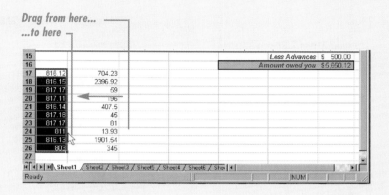

▶ The columns are transposed so that the account numbers are on the left, the expense totals on the right.

5 Click anywhere outside of the highlighted range, or press the **Esc** key, to turn off the highlight.

Sorting the Data

You can now sort the data in this two-column table you have added to the sheet.

1 Select the range **A17:B26** (all of the new table).

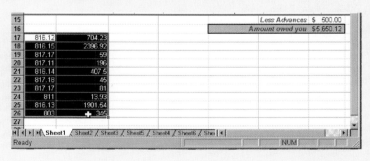

2 From the menu bar, select
Data ➤ Sort.

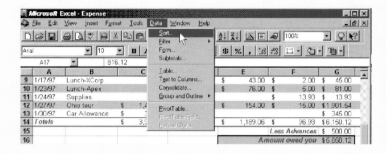

▶ The Sort dialog box will
appear.

▶ For any sorting operation,
you must specify the *sort
key,* a range according to
which the data in another
range will be sorted. In this
case, the key will be the
account numbers in column
A, by which expense totals
in column B will be sorted.
Since column A is preselected
in the Sort By text box, you
do not need to make any
further selections here.

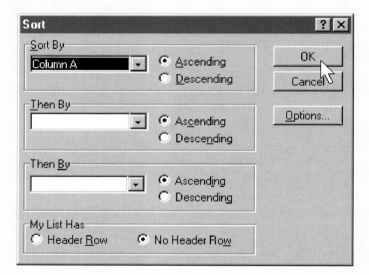

3 Click on **OK** to close the
dialog box and start the
sorting process.

▶ The expense totals in column B will be rearranged, sorted by the account numbers in column A, in ascending numeric order.

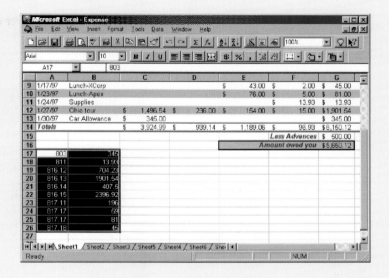

Calculating Account Totals

Before you apply appearance formatting to the table, you should calculate totals for each of the accounts.

1 Click on cell **C22**.

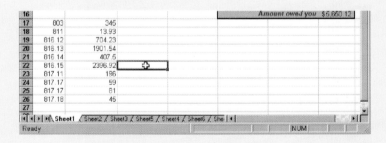

2 In the toolbar, click on the **AutoSum** tool.

3 Click and drag to select the range **B19:B22** (all of the 816 expense items).

4 Press ↵.

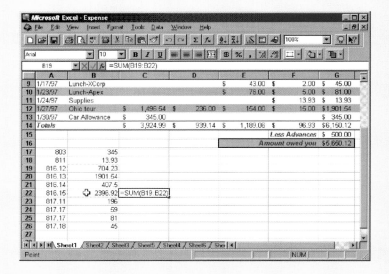

5 Now, use the same procedure to get the total of the 817 expenses: Start by clicking cell **C26**.

6 Click on the **AutoSum** tool.

7 Drag the range **B23:B26** and press ↵.

▶ Totals for accounts 816 and
817 will now appear in the
cells that hold the formulas
generated by AutoSum.

16				Amount owed you $5,650.12
17	803	345		
18	811	13.93		
19	816.12	704.23		
20	816.13	1901.54		
21	816.14	407.5		
22	816.15	2396.92	5410.19	
23	817.11	196		
24	817.17	59		
25	817.17	81		
26	817.18	45	381	
27				

Ready | NUM

Copying Data by Drag-and-Drop

Since the 803 and 811 accounts each have only one expense item, you can copy these
amounts into column C as totals. Use the drag-and-drop copying method, which is the
same as moving by dragging, except that you hold the Ctrl key down as you drag. Try
it now.

1 Click and drag to highlight
B17:B18 to select both
totals.

16			
17	803	345	— *Drag from here...*
18	811	13.93	
19	816.12	704.23	...*to here*
20	816.13	1901.54	
21	816.14	407.5	
22	816.15	2396.92	5410.19

2 Move the cell pointer to the
edge of your selection until
the pointer shape changes
to an arrowhead.

16			
17	803	345	
18	811	13.93	
19	816.12	704.23	
20	816.13	1901.54	
21	816.14	407.5	
22	816.15	2396.92	5410.19

123

3 Hold down **Ctrl** as you drag the highlighted cells from B17:B18 to C17:C18. (Notice that a plus sign (+) appears next to the pointer to indicate that the data is being copied rather than moved.)

16			
17	803	345	
18	811	13.93	
19	816.12	704.23	
20	816.13	1901.54	
21	816.14	407.5	
22	816.15	2396.92	5410.19

Hold down Ctrl and drag from here...   *...to here*

4 Release the mouse button.

▶ The selected data will be copied to the location where you released the mouse button.

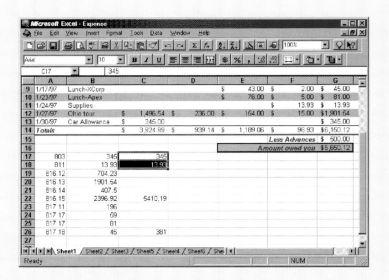

Formatting the Table

Now you can apply number and appearance formats to the table.

Applying the Currency Format

You need to apply the Currency number format to the second and third columns of the table.

1 Select the range B17:C26.

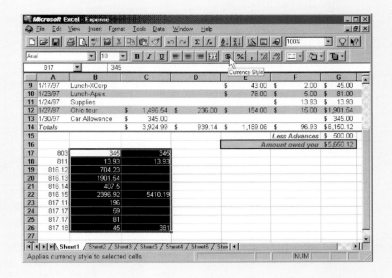

2 In the toolbar, click on the **Currency Style** tool.

▶ The expense totals will be displayed as dollar amounts.

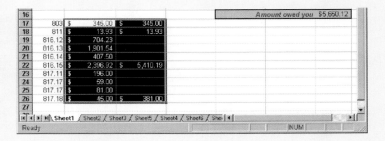

3 Press the **Esc** key. Click anywhere outside of the highlighted range to turn off the highlighting.

Underscoring Your Totals

There is a convention in accounting for showing totals by drawing an underscore beneath the values. You can do this in Excel by adding borders to the bottoms of selected cells.

1 While holding down **Ctrl**, click on the following cells: **C17**, **C18**, **C22**, and **C26**.

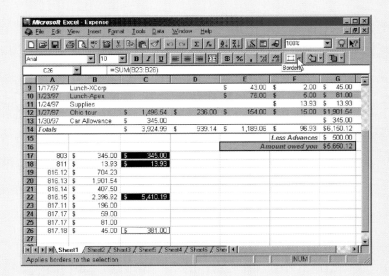

2 In the toolbar, click on the ↓ button next to the Borders button to open the **Borders** drop-down box.

3 Click on the **double-under-scored** border option.

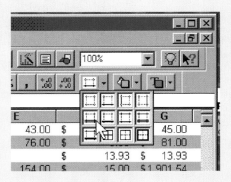

4 Click on any other cell to release the highlight from the selected cells.

▶ The double-underscore border appears on the selected cells, indicating totals for each major account category.

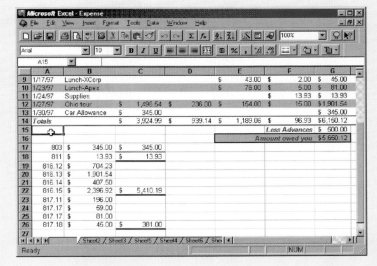

Previewing and Printing the Report

You can now preview and print the revised report.

1 In the toolbar, select the **Print Preview** tool.

▶ If you chose the Center Horizontally and Vertically options in Lesson 6, these should still be set, and the previewed report should look like this.

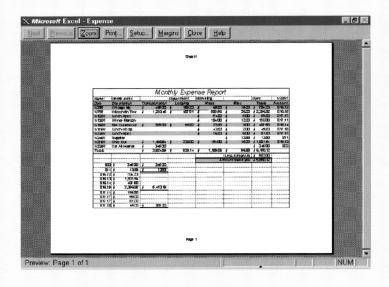

2 In Preview mode, select the **Print** button at the top of the screen.

3 The Print dialog box will appear. Click on **OK** to start printing.

> **NOTE**
> If you need help previewing or printing the report, review the steps in Lesson 6.

Saving Your Work

You have completed Lesson 7. Before proceeding to the next lesson, and particularly if you need to quit the program, save your work.

8 Creating a Worksheet Outline

The expense report that you have built up in previous lessons is a summary of expenditures for a month of business activities. Even though you show only summary totals in the report, you would normally be expected to keep detailed records to back up those totals. It would be convenient, then, to include the supporting information in the workbook file, yet be able to suppress it when the report is printed.

This is just one application of the Data ➤ Group And Outline command in Excel. In this lesson, you will add expense subtotals to the Expense sheet, then provide a way for displaying them selectively by outlining the sheet. You will also learn how to include text comments and notes in your worksheets.

Starting Excel and Opening the Workbook File

Recall that you were working with the document window maximized in Lessons 6 and 7. This puts as much of the sheet as possible on the screen at one time.

1   Begin this lesson by starting Excel and opening the **Expense** workbook. (If you need help, refer to the procedure at the beginning of Lesson 7.)

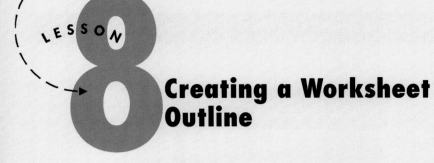

▶ The worksheet should appear in a maximized document window, as shown in the illustration. If not, click on the window's **Maximize** button.

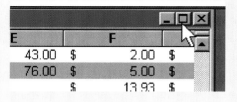

Inserting New Rows in the Sheet

In its present form, there is no place in the sheet for itemized expenses. Provide for these entries now by inserting two more rows within the existing sheet.

1 Click on the ↑ button on the vertical scroll bar several times until row 4 is displayed at the top of the window.

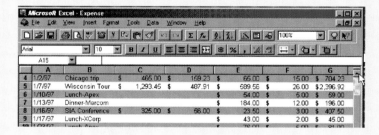

2 Click on cell **B5**, which holds the label "Wisconsin Tour."

3 From the menu bar, select **Insert ➤ Rows**.

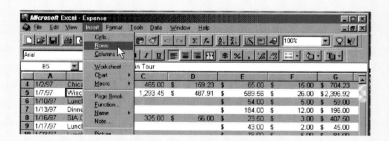

▶ A new, blank row will appear just above the selected cell. Note that all the rows below the new row have been moved down and renumbered as a result. The cell highlight has not moved. It is still in B5, which is now in the new row.

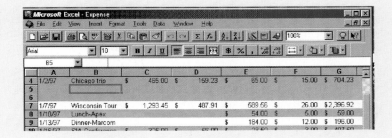

4 Without moving the cell highlight (it should remain in cell B5), repeat the **Insert ▶ Rows** command.

▶ Another blank row will be added to the sheet.

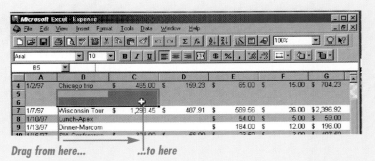

Itemizing Your Expenses

You now have two empty rows beneath the row of expense items for the Chicago trip. Use these rows to hold an itemization of your expenses.

1 Click and drag to select the range **B5:C6**.

Drag from here...   ...to here

2 Type the following data entries, pressing ↵ after each one: **Air fare, Car rental, 342, 123.**

	A	B	C
4	1/2/97	Chicago trip	$ 465.00 $
5		Air fare	$ 342.00
6		Car rental	$ 123.00
7	1/7/97	Wisconsin Tour	$ 1,293.45 $

Updating Formulas in the Sheet

For the sheet to be set up properly for automatic outlining, the amount in cell C4 must come from Excel performing a summary calculation using the new items you've entered (rather than simply displaying the amount you *entered* as a total). Provide for that now by using the AutoSum tool.

1 Click on cell **C4.**

	A	B	C
4	1/2/97	Chicago trip	$ 465.00 $
5		Air fare	$ 342.00
6		Car rental	$ 123.00
7	1/7/97	Wisconsin Tour	$ 1,293.45 $

2 In the toolbar, click on the **AutoSum** tool.

AutoSum tool

3 Drag the pointer so that the moving dotted line surrounds **C5:C6.**

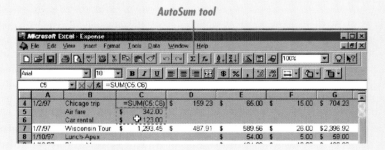

4 Click on ✓.

132

▶ Cell C4 now holds the formula =SUM(C5:C6) so that its entry is a true summary of the itemized expenses.

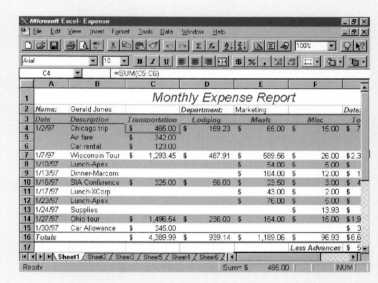

▶ However, the sheet as it is currently built will produce incorrect results: your new data entries have been erroneously included in the total figure in cell C16.

Redefining a Range

To exclude the subtotals so that the amount shown in cell C16 is calculated correctly, you must redefine the range called **Transport** by deleting it and then recreating it. Here's a quick and easy way to do this.

1 From the menu bar, select
Insert ➤ Name ➤ Define.

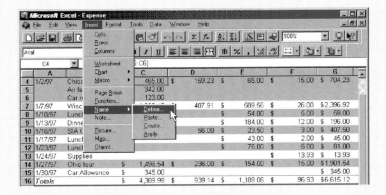

▶ The Define Name dialog
box will appear.

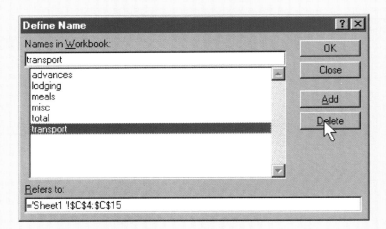

2 In the dialog box, click on
the name **transport**.

3 Click on the **Delete** button
in the dialog box.

4 Click on **OK** to close the
dialog box.

The range name Transport has now been removed from the sheet. You must now select
a new range of cells and recreate the name.

134

5 With cell **C4** (the topmost cell you want to include in the range) still selected, hold down **Ctrl** to select non-adjacent cells, and drag the pointer to select the range **C7:C15**.

Previously selected cell

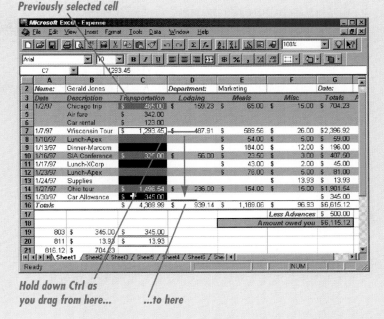

Hold down Ctrl as you drag from here... *...to here*

6 On the left side of the formula bar, click on the ↓ button next to the **Name box** to drop down a list of named cells in the worksheet.

7 Type **transport**.

8 Press ↵.

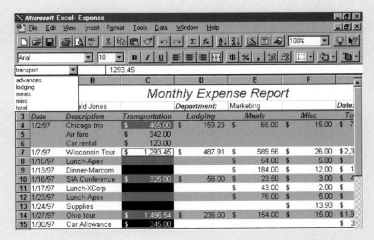

135

▶ The Transport range name has been redefined to contain the cell C4 and the range C7:C15, thus excluding the amounts in C5 and C6. The correct total is now shown in cell C16.

10	1/16/97	CIA Conference	$	525.00
11	1/17/97	Lunch-XCorp		
12	1/23/97	Lunch-Apex		
13	1/24/97	Supplies		
14	1/27/97	Ohio tour	$	1,496.54 $
15	1/30/97	Car Allowance	$	345.00 $
16	*Totals*		$	3,924.99 $
17				

Updated total

NOTE

These detailed expense entries are shown here to illustrate the Outline feature of Excel. If you actually use this sheet and insert other itemized expenses, you will have to follow similar steps to update any range names or formulas that might otherwise include them. That is, if you insert more rows and itemized expenses in the Transport, Lodging, Meals, and Misc ranges, you will have to redefine those range names so that the formulas in row 16 will generate correct column totals.

Creating an Outline

A worksheet outline makes selected rows or columns (or both) subordinate to other rows or columns in a sheet or workbook. The result is that the subordinate entries can be alternately displayed or hidden on command. Follow these steps to see how this works:

1 Click and drag to select the range **A4:G6**.

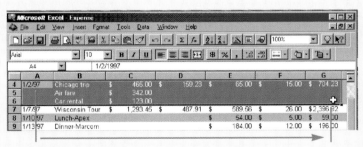

Drag from here...   ...to here

2 From the menu bar, select **Data ➤ Group And Outline ➤ Auto Outline**.

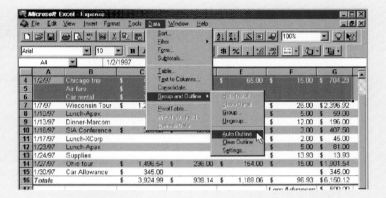

▶ The display will change to include buttons for manipulating the sheet as a multiple-level outline.

Column level symbols

Row level symbols

Collapse symbols

Controlling the Outline Display

At the left edge of the sheet will appear Row Level symbols labeled 1 and 2, as well as a Collapse symbol, which is labeled with a minus sign (–). These symbols are buttons that you can click on to control the display of the outline.

Hiding the Subordinate Rows

You can hide the subordinate rows, or collapse the outline, literally at the touch of a button. Try it now.

1   Click on the **Collapse** button.

		A	B	C
	4	1/2/97	Chicago trip	$ 465.0
	5		Air fare	$ 342.0
	6		Car rental	$ 123.0
	7	1/7/97	Wisconsin Tour	$ 1,293.4
	8	1/10/97	Lunch-Apex	

▶ The subordinate rows will be hidden, and the Collapse button will turn into an **Expand** button, labeled with a plus sign (+).

Expand symbol

		A	B	C	D	E	F	G
	4	1/2/97	Chicago trip	$ 465.00	$ 159.23	$ 65.00	$ 15.00	$ 704
	7	1/7/97	Wisconsin Tour	$ 1,293.45	$ 487.91	$ 589.56	$ 26.00	$2,396.
	8	1/10/97	Lunch-Apex			$ 54.00	$ 5.00	$ 59.
	9	1/13/97	Dinner-Marcom			$ 184.00	$ 12.00	$ 196.
	10	1/16/97	SIA Conference	$ 325.00	$ 56.00	$ 23.50	$ 3.00	$ 407.
	11	1/17/97	Lunch-XCorp			$ 43.00	$ 2.00	$ 45.
	12	1/23/97	Lunch-Apex			$ 76.00	$ 5.00	$ 81
	13	1/24/97	Supplies				$ 13.93	$ 13
	14	1/27/97	Ohio tour	$ 1,496.54	$ 238.00	$ 154.00	$ 15.00	$1,901.
	15	1/30/97	Car Allowance	$ 345.00				$ 345.
	16		Totals	$ 3,924.99	$ 939.14	$ 1,189.06	$ 96.93	$6,150.
	17						Less Advances	$ 500
	18						Amount owed you	$5,650
	19		803	$ 345.00	$ 345.00			
	20		811	$ 13.93	$ 13.93			
	21		816.12	$ 704.23				
	22		816.13	$ 1,901.54				

Revealing the Subordinate Rows

You can simply click on the **Expand** button to restore the outline to its expanded form, revealing the subordinate rows. As an alternative—especially if an outline includes multiple levels—you can click on the **Row Level** symbol of the view you want. In this case, the outline has two levels. Restore the original view of the sheet now.

1   Click on the Row Level symbol labeled **2**.

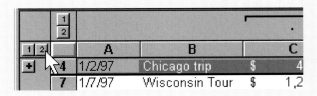

▶ The expanded sheet will reappear, including your itemized expenses for the Chicago trip.

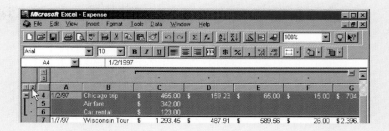

> **NOTE**
> Depending on the layout of a sheet, you may see buttons at the top of the window for collapsing/expanding the columns as well. You can control the *printing* of subordinate rows or columns the same way you control the display. Outlines are WYSIWYG (What You See Is What You Get), which means the printout will match the screen display.

Annotating the Sheet with Text

You might also want to add text comments or notes in a worksheet. There are two kinds of annotations: *text boxes* that are printed with the document, and *text notes* that are included in the file but are hidden from view until you want them.

Adding a Text Box

A text box is an annotation to a sheet that will normally be printed out. However, because you have created an outline in this sheet, you can add a reminder to yourself that will be printed only if you print the outline in its expanded form. The trick to doing this is in placing the text box in a subordinate entry in the outline.

1 Right-click your mouse on any toolbar to bring up the toolbar shortcut menu.

2 Select the **Drawing toolbar**.

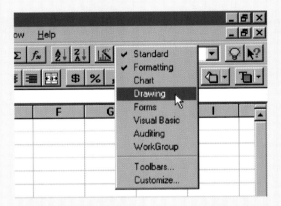

3 In the Drawing toolbar select the **Text Box** tool.

▶ The pointer will change to a small cross.

4 In rows 5 and 6 of the sheet, click and drag within the range **D5:E6** to create a box that will hold the text.

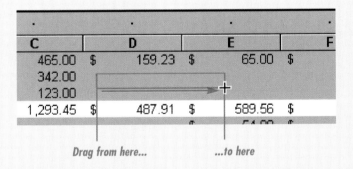

Drag from here...   *...to here*

▶ When you release the mouse button, a flashing I-beam cursor will appear inside the box.

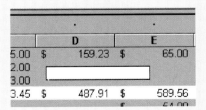

5 Type **Cash for gas: $14.95**.

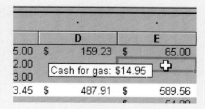

6 Click anywhere outside the text box.

▶ The text box now contains a reminder of your cash expenditure.

Because the text is contained within the subordinate rows of the outline, it will not be visible when the outline is collapsed. However, if the outline is shown in expanded mode when the sheet is printed, the text box will be printed as well.

Adding a Text Note

Unlike a text *box*, a text *note* is an annotation that will appear only on screen, and even then only when you want to see it, and will not be printed with the sheet. Add a note now that will help to document the way you built this sheet.

1 Click on cell **A5**.

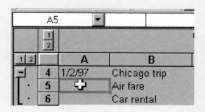

2 From the menu bar, select **Insert ➤ Note**.

▶ The Cell Note dialog box will appear.

3 In the Text Note box of this dialog box, type the following:

> If subordinate rows are added, be sure to update all affected range names and
> formulas!

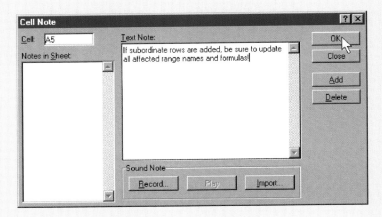

4 Click on **OK** to close the dialog box.

▶ A small red dot will appear in the top right corner of the cell that contains the note. (The dot will not show when the sheet is pre-viewed or printed.)

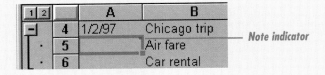

Note indicator

Viewing Text Notes

A worksheet can contain many notes, one in each cell. There are various ways to view notes after you have added them to a sheet, as described here.

▶ Select Insert ➤ Note, then, in the Cell Note dialog box, click on the cell whose note you want to read (they're listed in the Notes In Sheet list box on the left side of the dialog box). When you are finished reading the notes, click on the Close button.

▶ You can also view notes by letting the pointer linger for a moment on a cell that displays a note indicator, and a pop up note will appear.

NOTE

You can turn the display of note indicators on and off by selecting Tools ➤ Options from the menu bar and then, on the View tab page, clicking on the Note Indicator checkbox.

Saving Your Work

All the features you have added to the Expense sheet—the outline, text box, and note—will be saved in the workbook file and will be available whenever you reopen it. Before you exit Excel, and while the Expense sheet is open and active, save the file.

LESSON

9 Linking Worksheets in a Workbook

10 MINUTES

There will be times when you want to transfer results from one worksheet to another. It would be most convenient if you could have the program do this for you, without your having to reenter the data. With Excel for Windows, you can link worksheets to share data. Updates will be automatic, so a change in one sheet will affect all the others to which it is linked. (You can also share data among Windows applications, but that topic is beyond the scope of this book.)

In accounting, for example, the need for data links arises when you must carry the results of a supporting schedule to a ledger. In the expense report example, it will be necessary to carry the expense totals from individual expense reports to a management-level report that summarizes expenses for your department.

In this lesson, you will build a portion of the department summary sheet, then link it to your own expense sheet. To make it easy to access both sheets, you can create and store them in a single workbook file. Recall that, in Excel, a workbook file can hold many related worksheets.

Starting Excel and Opening the Sheet

Begin this lesson by starting Excel and opening the Expense workbook. Select the file name from the File menu, or use the Open File tool. If you need help, refer to the procedure at the beginning of Lesson 7.

144

▶ The workbook will be opened in the maximized document window, showing the outlined version of Sheet1, which holds your expense report for the month of January.

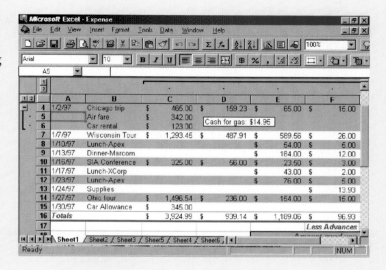

For your work with the expense report in this lesson, you can use the outlined sheet in compact, collapsed form—showing only expense descriptions and totals. Collapse the sheet now.

1 In the Column Level buttons just above the row numbers, click **1**.

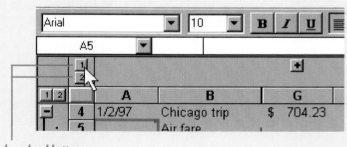

Column level buttons

2 To hide the rows that hold your itemized expenses and notes for the Chicago trip, in the Row Level buttons to the left of the column letters, click **1**.

3 Click the ↑ button on the vertical scroll bar several times until the title of the report is shown.

▶ The outlined sheet will be displayed in its most collapsed view, showing only dates, descriptions, totals, and account numbers.

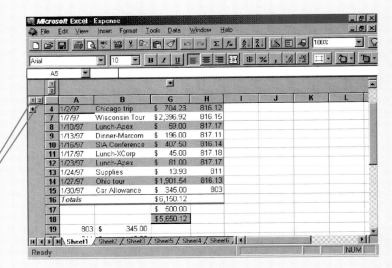

Row level buttons

Preparing Multiple Sheets

Because the two sheets you will be using in this lesson both relate to company expenses, it will be convenient to build and store them in the same workbook file you've already opened.

Renaming a Sheet

Before you start a new sheet, rename Sheet1 so that you will know from a glance at its index tab what it contains.

1 At the bottom of the document window, double-click the index tab **Sheet1**. The Rename Sheet dialog box will appear.

2 Type **January Expenses**.

3 Press ↵ (or select OK) to close the dialog box.

▶ The new sheet name will appear in its index tab.

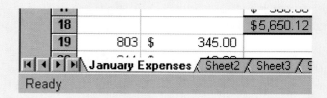

Starting a New Sheet

In any workbook, you can activate a new sheet simply by clicking any of the available index tabs. Do this now.

1 Among the index tabs at the bottom of the document window, click **Sheet2**.

147

▶ A blank sheet will open, as if it were moved to the top of the stack of sheets, covering the expense report, which is now visible only by its dimmed index tab.

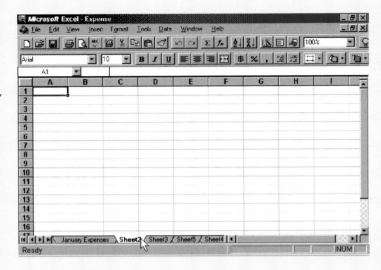

Building a Departmental Summary

Use this new sheet to build a summary report that will recap the expenses for all staff members in your department. Start by renaming the sheet.

Renaming the Summary Sheet

Use the procedure just described to rename Sheet2 **Dept. Summary.**

Entering Column Headings

Begin to build the new sheet by entering its column labels.

1 Click and drag to highlight the range **A2:C2.**

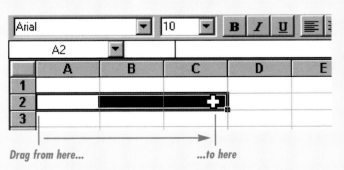

Drag from here...   ...to here

2 Type **Employee**, **Date**, **Expenses** (pressing ↵ after each entry).

3 Click the **Center** tool.

▶ The labels will appear in the row you selected, centered over the columns.

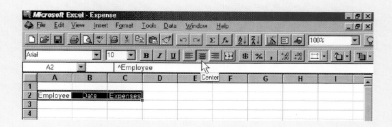

Viewing Two Sheets at the Same Time

You can have several sheets—even several workbooks—open at the same time in Excel. (The only limitation is the amount of memory in your computer.) In preparation for transferring data from your expense report to the summary sheet, rearrange the sheets now so that you can see both of them.

Arranging Sheets

Follow these steps so that you can display and work on both sheets at the same time. Start by opening a window in which the other sheet can be displayed.

1 From the menu bar, select **Window ➤ New Window**.

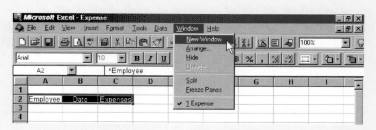

2 Also from the menu bar, select **Window ➤ Arrange**.

▶ The Arrange Windows dialog box will appear.

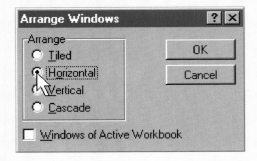

3 From the Arrange options, select **Horizontal**.

4 Select **OK** to close the dialog box.

▶ Two document windows will be shown. The windows are identified as Expense:1 and Expense:2, the labels appearing in the title bars. However, note that only one of the title bars is highlighted, indicating that this is the active window. (Only one window can be active at a time, and scroll bars will appear only in that window.)

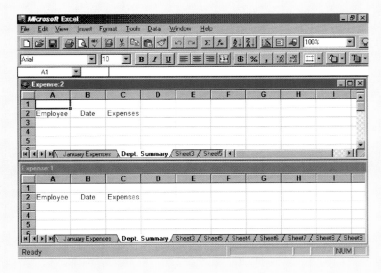

Activating the Expense Sheet

Now, activate the lower window and switch its display to the expense report:

1 In window 1, click the **January Expenses** index tab. The title bar of the window becomes highlighted. (You could have clicked anywhere within the window.)

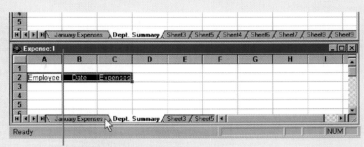

Highlighted title bar indicates active window.

2 Click the **January Expenses** index tab again. The display in the lower window will change to show the expense report.

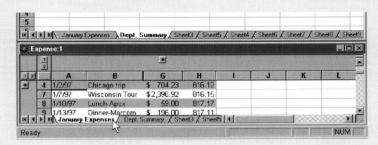

3 Click the ↑ button in the vertical scroll bar several times until cell B2 (which holds your name) is shown.

4 In preparation for the next step, click cell **B2** to select it.

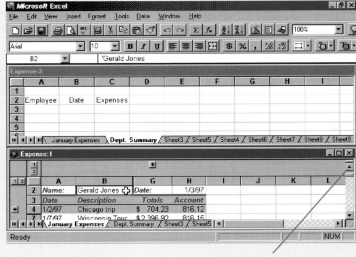

Click to scroll the sheet.

Creating a Data Link

All of the entries you need to show in the Dept. Summary sheet from your own expense report are already contained in the January Expense sheet. With both sheets open, you need only copy the data from one sheet to the other, creating an ongoing data link in the process.

Using the Paste Link Feature

Transfer your name now, using the Paste Link feature to create the link.

1 Having selected cell B2, click the right mouse button. A shortcut menu will appear.

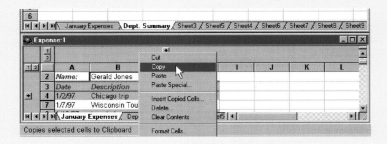

2 From the shortcut menu, select **Copy**.

▶ A moving dotted line will surround the selected cell, indicating that its contents have been copied to the Windows Clipboard.

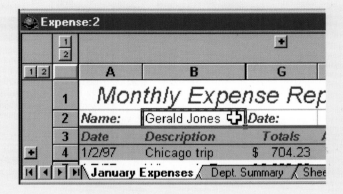

3 Move the pointer into the top window (2) and click cell **A4** twice (not a double-click, but two single clicks—one to activate the sheet, one to select the cell).

4 Click the right mouse button to activate a shortcut menu.

153

5 From the shortcut menu, select **Paste Special**.

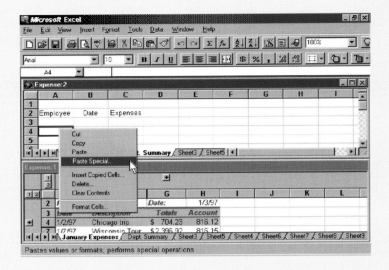

▶ The Paste Special dialog box will appear.

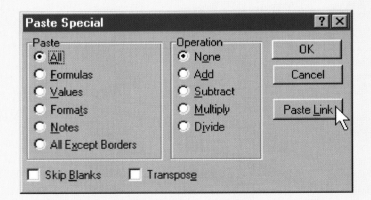

6 In the dialog box, click the **Paste Link** button.

7 Press **Esc** to release cell B2.

154

▶ Your name will be pasted into cell A4, along with a data link by which any update will affect both sheets.

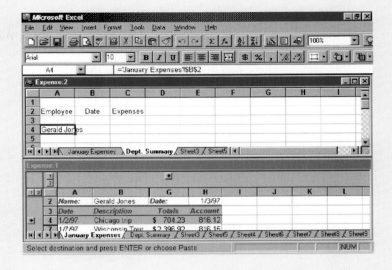

NOTE

The shortcut menu selections described here are equivalent to selecting **Edit ➤ Copy** and **Edit ➤ Paste Special ➤ Paste Link** from the menu bar.

Verifying the Data Link

With cell A4 still selected, look at the contents of the formula bar:

    ='January Expenses'!B2

This formula, or *link reference*, indicates the source of the linked data. The formula symbol, the equal sign (=), is followed by the sheet name 'January Expenses'. (If you had taken the data from a different open workbook file, the file name—enclosed in brackets—would precede the sheet name.) After the sheet name in the formula, notice the exclamation point (!), or link symbol, and the address of the cell that holds the data (B2). The dollar signs indicate that the column letter and row number of the address are *absolute*, or can't be readjusted by the program, even if the sheet is rearranged.

> **NOTE**
> If you do not see a link reference in the formula bar after you perform the Paste Link pro-
> cedure, a link was not established. You should check to be sure that you are requesting a
> valid link, then try it again.

Creating Other Links

There can be multiple links between sheets, so you can let the program do the work of entering the rest of the required items from your report.

1   Move the pointer into the lower sheet (1), and select cell **H2**. This cell holds the date of your report.

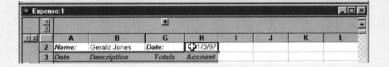

2   Click the right mouse button to activate a shortcut menu.

3   From the shortcut menu, select **Copy**.

4   In the top sheet, click cell **B4**. (For now, don't be concerned if your name in cell A4 overlaps this cell.)

5 Click the right mouse button to activate a shortcut menu.

6 From the shortcut menu, select **Paste Special**. The Paste Special dialog box will appear.

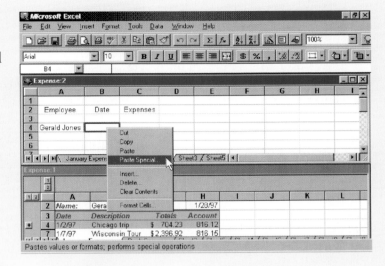

7 In the dialog box, click **Paste Link**.

8 Press **Esc**.

▶ A linked copy of the report date will be pasted into cell B4 of the Dept. Summary sheet.

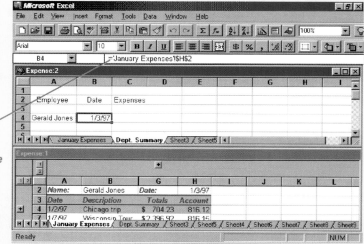

Formula bar shows link reference

9 Click the title bar of the lower sheet **Expense 1** to activate it.

10 Click the ↓ button on the vertical scroll bar several times until cell G16 (the expense total before deducting advances) is displayed.

11 Click cell **G16**.

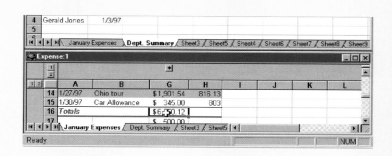

12 Repeat the **Copy**, **Paste Special**, and **Paste Link** procedures to paste a linked copy of the data into cell **C4** of the Dept. Summary sheet.

13 Press **Esc**.

▶ A linked copy of the data will appear as the overflow indicator (######) in cell C4, indicating that the cell is not wide enough to display the value.

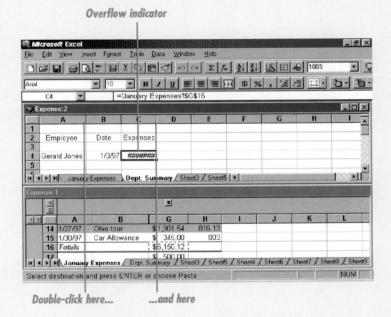

Overflow indicator

Double-click here...   *...and here*

14 To adjust the display of the Dept. Summary sheet to increase the widths of columns A and C, double-click on the right borders of each of those column headings.

▶ The Dept. Summary sheet now holds all of the data required from your expense report.

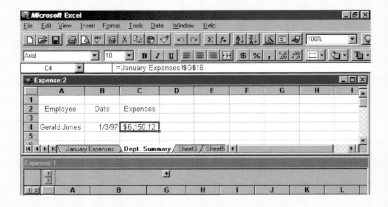

Using Linked Worksheets

The two open sheets now share three data items. Because those items are linked, making a change to an item in one sheet will affect the corresponding item in the other.

Making Updates

You can see for yourself how data links operate. Try this now.

1 Click the title bar of **EXPENSE:1** to activate the sheet. (Again, you can click anywhere in the sheet, but it's always safe to click on the title bar.)

Click here to activate the sheet

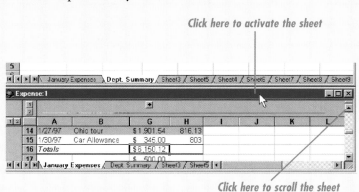

Click here to scroll the sheet

2 Click the ↑ button on the vertical scroll bar several times until cell H2 (the date) is displayed.

3 Click cell **H2**.

4 Type **1-28-97**.

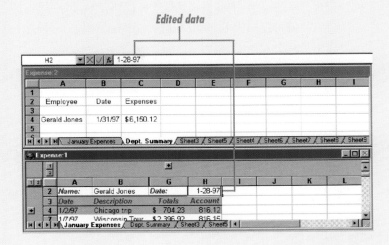

Edited data

5 Press ↵.

▶ The date will be changed in both cell H2 of sheet 1 and in cell B4 of sheet 2.

Editing H2 also updates B4 in the linked sheet.

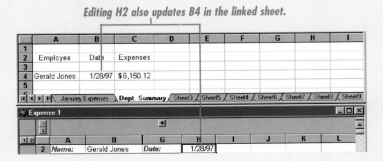

Linking Other Sheets

You could open other sheets—perhaps in different workbooks containing the expense reports of other employees—and link them to the department just as you did here to create a report for an entire work group.

161

> **NOTE**
> If you open a file that contains a link to another file that is closed, the program will ask you whether the link should be updated: "Update references to unopened documents? (Yes or No)."

Controlling Document Windows

Although you have worked with sheets 1 and 2 in separate document windows in this lesson, remember that they are contained in the same workbook (Expense). If you were to save your work now, with both windows showing, this is exactly how the sheets would appear when you reopened the file. However, perhaps you would rather see your expense report filling the screen when the file is opened. Here's how to control the document windows.

1 Click the title bar of the top sheet (2) to activate it.

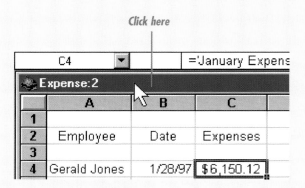

Click here

2 Click the **Control** of sheet 2 in its top left corner.

▶ The window's control menu will appear.

Control

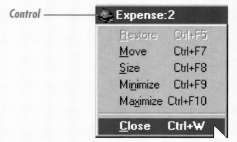

3 From the control menu, select **Close**.

▶ You can also close a window by clicking on the **X** control in the upper right hand corner of the window.

▶ The document window for sheet 2 will disappear from the screen.

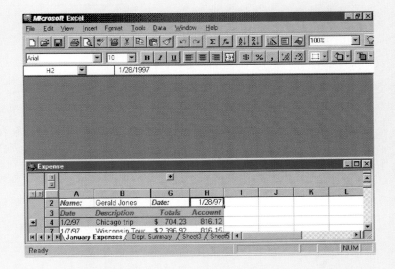

4 Click the **Maximize** button in the top right corner of the open sheet.

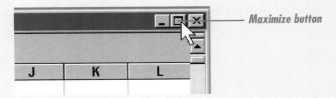

Maximize button

163

▶ The document window that holds the January Expenses sheet will be enlarged to fill the screen. Whenever you wish to view the Dept. Summary sheet, just click its index tab at the bottom of the window.

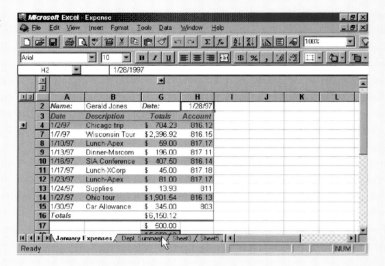

NOTE

This is one instance in Excel when closing a window is not the same as closing a file. The second window is just an alternate view of the same file you are working with in the other window. So, when you close the alternate view, the program will not ask if you want to save your changes, because the file is still open. (As an alternative to selecting **Close** from the control menu, you can simply double-click the window's control box.)

Save It!

Before you go on to the next lesson or exit Excel, save the file. Both sheets will be saved in the workbook Expense.

10

Charting and Mapping

15 MINUTES

If you have worked through the lessons to this point, you already know how to build and format a fully functional worksheet, and how to print it out. In short, you have all the skills you need to get useful results from Excel for Windows 95. Beyond the basics, however, the program includes a wealth of other powerful tools, which are just too numerous to include in this short book.

This lesson can serve as an introduction to this wider world of Excel. You will work with one of the program's most popular features: the ChartWizard. And, along the way, you will also discover some other handy uses of AutoFill.

Starting Excel and Opening the Sheet

Begin this lesson by starting Excel. There is no need to open a file. You will be working in the default document window Book1, which should open automatically when you start the program. (If you have not changed the settings from the previous lesson, the document window will be maximized. If you want your screens to match the illustrations in this lesson exactly, click its **Restore** button.)

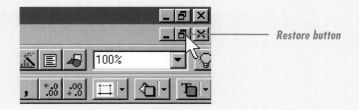

Restore button

Building a Table for Charting

Just about any worksheet you create can be charted, but the real question becomes: What makes a meaningful chart? Ideally, a chart should highlight relationships in the data that might be difficult to see in the tabular form of a worksheet.

In the following steps, you will build a table that breaks down the hours you might spend doing specific tasks in a typical workweek. Charting these data should highlight the tasks that might be taking up too much of your time.

Entering Labels

Begin to build the sheet by entering its title, column headings, and row labels.

1 Click cell **A1**.

2 Type **Productivity Study**

3 Click the ✔ button.

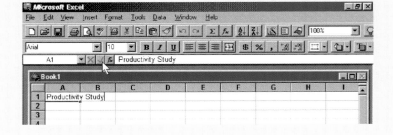

4 Click and drag to highlight the row **A1:F1**, which contains the text you just entered.

5 Click the **Center Across Columns** tool.

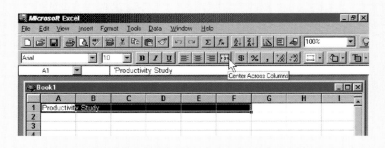

6 Click and drag to highlight the row **B2:F2**.

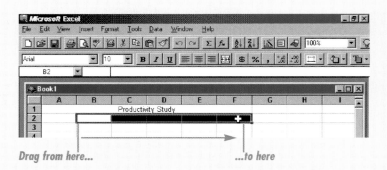

Drag from here...   ...to here

7 Type the following entries, pressing ⏎ after each: **Phone, Mail, Filing, Meetings, Other**.

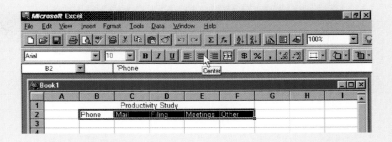

8 Click the **Center** tool.

9 Click cell **A3**.

10 Type **Mon**.

11 Click the ✓ button.

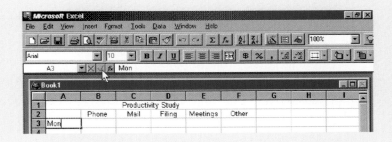

Using AutoFill to Increment Values

You have entered an abbreviation for Monday in cell A3. Now use a handy feature of AutoFill to generate the rest of the days of the week automatically.

1 With cell A3 still selected, move the pointer to the fill handle (in the bottom-right corner of the cell highlight). The pointer will change to a solid plus sign.

2 Drag the plus sign from **A3** to **A7** and release the mouse button.

Taking its cue from your first entry (Mon), the program will fill in the other days of the week.

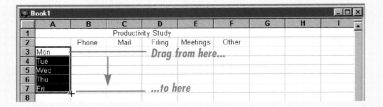

Remember this handy feature of AutoFill! Dragging the fill handle when the first cell contains calendar data—whether names or dates—will generate a valid sequence instead of merely copying the item.

NOTE

In some cases, it will be necessary to provide the first two items in the series. If you do this with specific dates, even end-of-month dates will be generated properly. For example, if you enter 2/28/97 and 3/31/97, the program will correctly set the next item to 4/30/97.

Entering the Data

You can use this same feature of AutoFill to generate estimates and projections. Try this now to estimate the number of hours spent on the phone.

1 Click and drag to highlight the range **B3:B4**.

2 Type **2.6** and **2.1**, pressing ↵ after each.

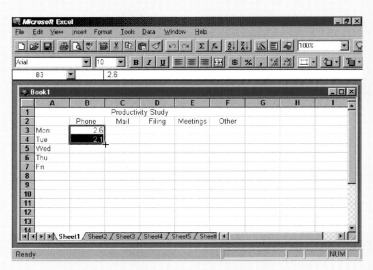

3 With the range still selected, move the pointer to the fill handle and drag it to **B7**.

4 Release the mouse button.

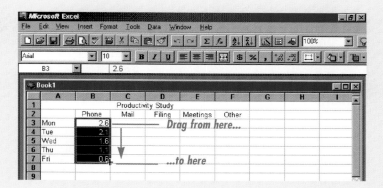

Notice what happened. The second data item you entered differs from the first by 0.5. When you used AutoFill, the program lowered the values of the following items in the series by this amount.

This automatic projection feature of AutoFill works best when the series of data items follows a *linear trend* (that is, when it increases or decreases steadily). However, your work patterns probably don't follow such convenient trends.

Completing the Data Entries

Enter the rest of the actual data in the sheet now, *overwriting* the linear projections.

1 Click and drag to highlight the range **B5:B7**.

2 Type **2.1**, **2.8**, and **2.4**, pressing ↵ after each.

These entries replace the ones you generated with AutoFill.

3 Click and drag to highlight the range **C3:F7**.

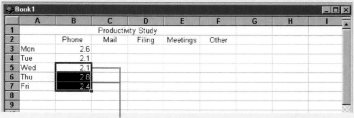

4 Type the following entries, pressing ↵ after each: **1.2, 0.8, 1.3, 1.5, 2.1, 0.4, 0.6, 0.8, 0.7, 1, 2.5, 3, 2.4, 2, 2.2, 1.4, 1.6, 1.4, 0.6,** and **0.4.**

Formatting the Sheet

Now that you've built the sheet, you might as well take a quick-and-easy step to make it more attractive.

1 Click and drag to highlight the range **A1:F7** (the whole table, including its title and headings).

2 From the menu bar, select **Format ➤ AutoFormat**.

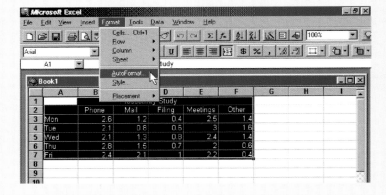

▶ The AutoFormat dialog box will appear.

3 In the Table Format options, select **Colorful 2**.

4 Click **OK** to close the dialog box.

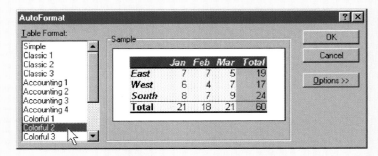

5 Click outside the range to release the selection and view the sheet in its new colors.

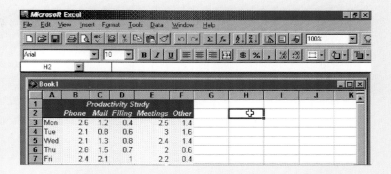

Saving the Sheet

Before you go any further, it would be a good idea to save the sheet to disk. This way, even if you make an error later, you can always select File ➤ Close, abandon the erroneous changes, and reopen a completed worksheet.

1 In the toolbar, click the **Save** tool.

▶ Because this is the first time you have saved this workbook, the Save As dialog box will appear.

2 Type **time** in the File name box and click **Save**.

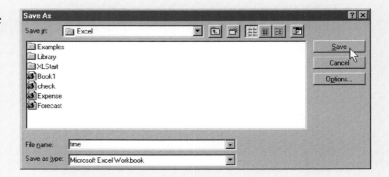

▶ The Properties dialog box will appear with the Summary tab selected.

3 In the Title box, type **Productivity Study**.

4 Click **OK** to close the dialog box.

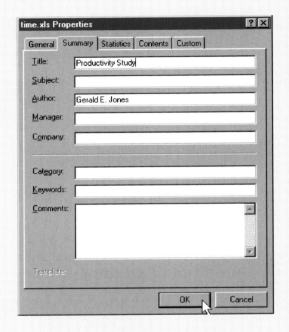

The workbook will be saved to disk in the file TIME.

NOTE

The fields in the Summary page—Title, Subject, Author, Manager, Company, Keywords, Category, and Comments—are provided to help you manage large numbers of files, typically in a workgroup situation in which you are sharing them with other staff members. To enter, view, or edit this information for any open Excel file, select File ➤ Properties from the menu bar, and this dialog box will reopen.

Using the ChartWizard to Generate a Chart

Excel provides the ChartWizard tool for generating charts. Try it now to plot the data from the productivity study.

NOTE

Any Excel feature that ends with the Wizard name is designed to greatly simplify the steps required for an otherwise complex procedure. Also included with the program is PivotTable Wizard, which helps you recompose, combine, and summarize tables.

1 Click and drag to highlight the range **A2:F7** (the whole sheet *except* its title).

2 Click the **ChartWizard** tool.

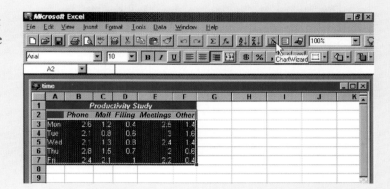

▶ A moving dotted line will appear around the selected range, and the pointer will change to cross hairs.

Cross-hairs pointer

3 Create an area in the sheet to hold the chart: Drag the cross hairs from the left edge of **G2** to the right edge of **K16**.

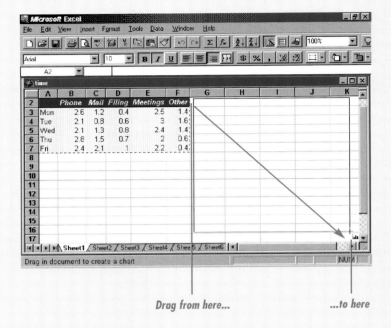

Drag from here...   *...to here*

▶ The first of five dialog boxes will appear: ChartWizard - Step 1 of 5. The range reference for the data you selected appears in its Range text box.

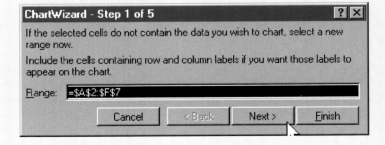

4 In the Step 1 dialog box, click **Next** to accept the range shown and advance to the next step.

▶ The Step 2 dialog box will appear, showing a variety of chart types.

5 To use the default setting, Column, click **Next**.

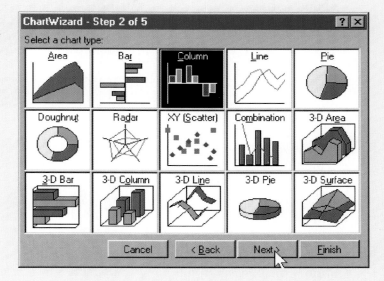

▶ The Step 3 dialog box will appear, showing format options for Column charts.

6 In this case, you need to reset the option. Click on chart **#3** (Stacked Columns).

7 Click **Next**.

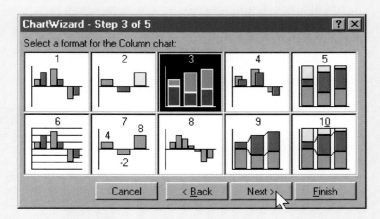

175

▶ The Step 4 dialog box will appear, containing a preview of the chart so far, along with some other option settings.

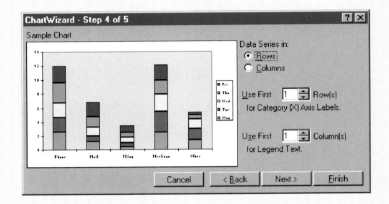

8 You'll need to change this setting to make a more meaningful chart. Select the Data Series In **Columns** option button.

▶ As soon as you select the option, the preview of the chart will change to show the result.

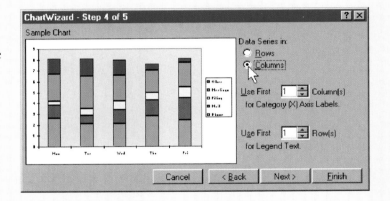

9 This is the chart you want, so click **Next**.

▶ The Step 5 dialog box will appear, in which you can enter titles for the chart and its axes.

10 Leave the Add A Legend? option set to Yes. Click in the Chart Title text box and type **Productivity Study**. (Do *not* press ↵.)

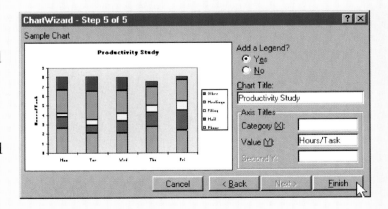

176

11 Press **Tab** *twice* to advance to the Value box (skipping the Category box).

12 Type **Hours/Task**.

13 Click **Finish** to close the Step 5 dialog box.

▶ The completed chart will appear in the sheet, surrounded by handles (small squares), indicating that the chart as a whole is currently selected for moving or resizing. (To give you more workspace, drag the floating Chart toolbar to the toolbar area.)

14 Click the **Save** tool to update the file TIME to include the chart.

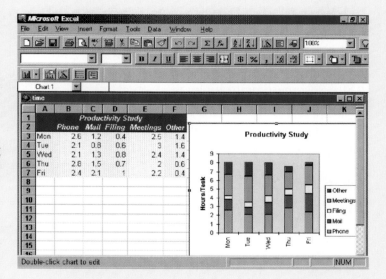

In just a few steps, you have generated a chart that is both attractive and meaningful. You can now see at a glance just where your valuable time is going!

NOTE

If the data series to be plotted are organized in rows (instead of columns as in this example), you can generate a default chart quickly simply by selecting Finish in the Step 1 of 5 dialog box (shown in step 4 above). Also, you can preview or print a chart just as you would any sheet. Select File ➤ Print Preview or File ➤ Print.

Finishing the Chart

The data entries in the table are linked to the chart. So, if you update the table, the chart will change accordingly.

But, after you created the data table, perhaps there was some data from the study that you overlooked completely. There's no need to repeat the ChartWizard steps. Here's how to include other data ranges in the plot.

Adding Chart Data with Drag-and-Drop

Once you have created a chart, you can drag other data ranges into it. The program will then replot the chart automatically, including the new data. Try this now.

1 Click and drag to highlight the row **A8:F8**.

2 Type the following data items, pressing ↵ after each one: **Sat, 1.5, 0.25, 0, 0,** and **0.5**.

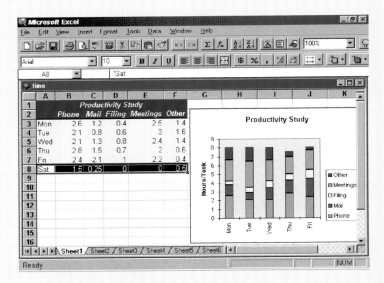

3 Move the cell pointer to any edge of the highlighted row. Its shape will change to an arrow.

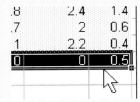
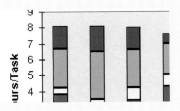

4 Drag the arrow pointer into the chart area. A small plus sign will appear with the arrow-shaped pointer, indicating that data will be added to the chart.

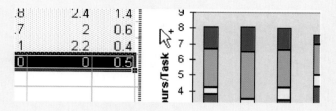

5 Release the mouse button.

▶ The chart will be replotted with the new data.

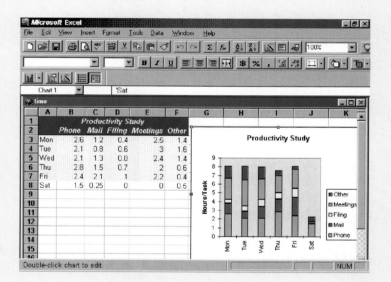

Using the Format Painter Tool

The row you added to the table doesn't have appearance formatting to match the other rows. Fix that now using the Format Painter tool.

1 Click and drag to highlight the row **A7:F7**, which has the formatting you want.

2 In the toolbar, click the **Format Painter** tool.

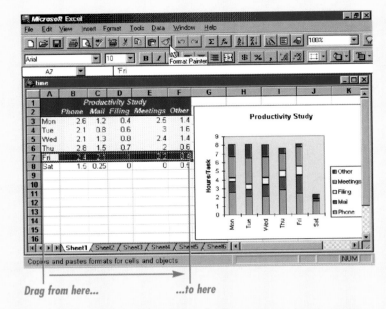

Drag from here...   ...to here

▶ A moving, dotted line will surround the selected cells and the cell pointer shape will change to a hollow plus sign with a paint brush.

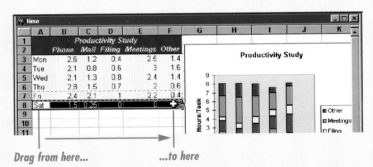

Drag from here...   ...to here

3 Drag the paint-brush pointer to select the row **A8:F8** (the row to which the formatting will be copied).

4 Release the mouse button.

5 Click any cell outside the table.

▶ The last row will match the rest of the table.

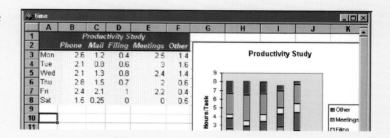

Editing a Chart

Excel for Windows contains an extensive set of tools for manipulating charts of many different types. Try experimenting with just a few of these features.

Selecting a Chart for Resizing or Moving

As with any other type of object in Excel, a chart must be selected before you can do commands that will change its appearance.

1 To select the chart for moving or resizing, click it once.

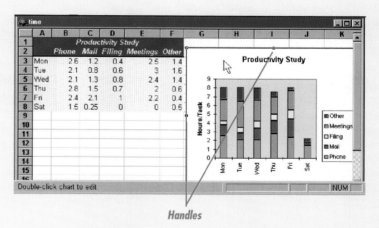

Handles

181

▶ A single set of handles, or small, black squares, will surround the chart.

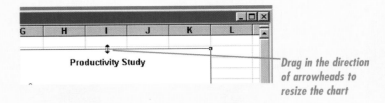

Drag in the direction of arrowheads to resize the chart

2 Drag any handle to resize the chart area.

3 Release the mouse button when the chart is the correct new size.

4 Click and drag on any point within the chart to move the whole chart.

5 Release the mouse button.

Drag to move the whole chart

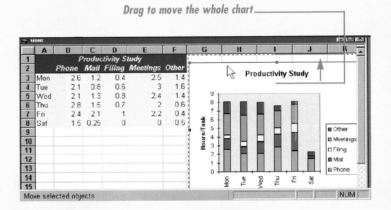

▶ The chart will appear in the new position.

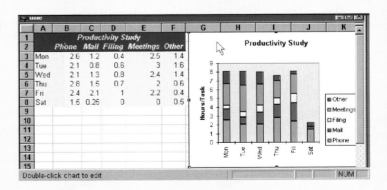

Selecting a Chart for Editing its Appearance

To change the appearance of a chart, you must perform a different type of selection.

1 Double-click any point inside the chart border.

▶ Another set of handles, as well as a bold colored border, will surround the chart. The larger set of handles indicates that the entire chart, rather than one of its elements, has been selected for editing.

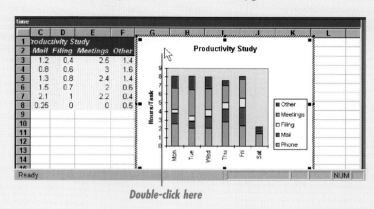

Double-click here

Adding Grid Lines to a Chart

Having selected the whole chart for editing, try changing one of its attributes—grid lines.

1 Click the right mouse button.

▶ A shortcut menu will appear.

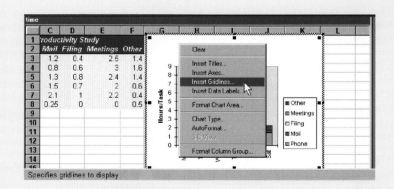

2 From the shortcut menu, select **Insert Gridlines**.

▶ The Gridlines dialog box
will appear.

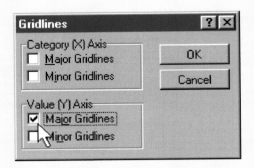

3 For this example, select the
Major Gridlines option for
the Value (Y) Axis.

4 Click **OK** to close the dialog box.

▶ Horizontal grid lines will
appear in the chart, indicating the major divisions of
the *y*-axis scale.

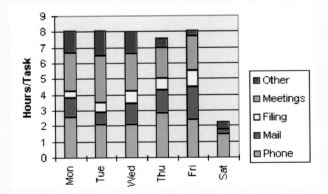

Changing the Chart Type

It might be more dramatic to display the data in a different type of chart. You can do
this with the AutoFormat feature.

1 With the entire chart still
selected for editing, click
the right mouse button.

▶ A shortcut menu will
appear.

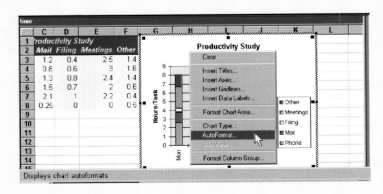

2 From the shortcut menu, select **AutoFormat**.

▶ The AutoFormat dialog box will appear.

3 In the dialog box, from the Galleries list, select **Area**.

▶ A selection of area chart formats will appear in the dialog box. The preselected option (4) will work nicely here.

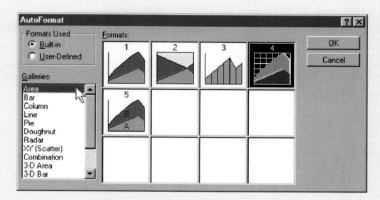

4 Click **OK** to close the dialog box.

▶ The column chart will be replotted as an area chart.

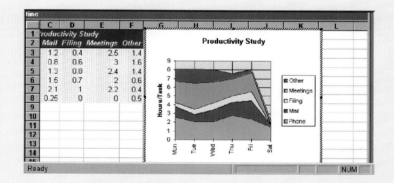

NOTE

Whenever a chart is selected for editing, you can select an object within it for individual editing simply by double-clicking the object. The selection is indicated by another set of handles that surrounds the object. For example, you could double-click a chart area and change its color in the Format Data Series dialog box that appears.

5 In the shortcut menu, there will be checks by the toolbars that are already in view. You can close Chart by selecting it if it is checked.

> **NOTE**
> You can move the Chart toolbar around the screen by dragging its title bar.

Remember that changing the chart style just presents a different view of the same data. In the example in this lesson, the areas are just as effective as the stacked columns in showing the relationships. However, depending on the information you are trying to present, some of the available chart types might not be appropriate or meaningful.

Creating a Map

The new mapping feature of Excel for Windows 95 lets you generate color-coded geographic maps from worksheet data—in much the same way you would create a chart. Try this now by adding a new sheet to the **Time** document.

Organizing Map Data

As with charts Excel assumes that data values for each region of a chart are organized in rows. If your table is laid out with the data in columns, select **Edit ➤ Paste Special ➤ Transpose** to rearrange the table, then create a map.

Start by creating a table of map data:

1 Click on the **Sheet2** tab.

▶ A blank sheet opens.

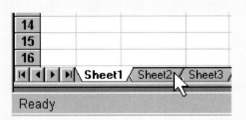

2 Click and drag to highlight the range **A1:B12**.

3 Type the following labels and values, pressing ↵ after each one: **State, AZ, CA, CO, ID, MT, NM, NV, OR, UT, WA, WY, Claims per 1000, 6, 8, 7, 3, 2, 5, 3, 2, 6, 3,** and **2.**

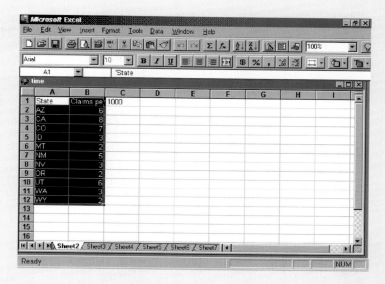

Notice how this table is built: Standard, two-letter abbreviations for states are in column A, numbers of customer complaints per thousand units shipped are in column B. Each row of the table contains a label and a corresponding value, and each row will be represented by one region of the map.

Generating a Map

Organizing your data according to this example can make quick work of the mapping process. Most important, the labels of the geographic regions should be standard names (such as **Arizona**) or abbreviations (such as **AZ**). (The names need not be in alphabetical order, however.)

If the program can recognize the region labels, it can generate the map automatically.

1 Click and drag to highlight the range **A2:B12** (all of the map data, *excluding* the column headings).

187

2 From the menu bar, select **Insert ➤ Map**.

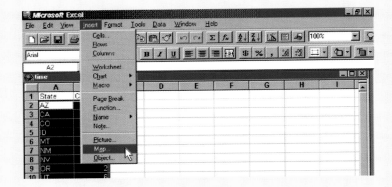

➤ The pointer shape changes to a small crosshair.

3 Click the middle of cell **C3** and drag the crosshair pointer to cell **H16**.

➤ The Multiple Maps Available dialog box appears.

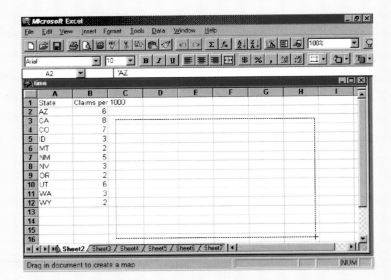

4 From the list, select **United States (AK & HI Insets)** in **United States with AK & HI Insets.**

5 Click **OK.**

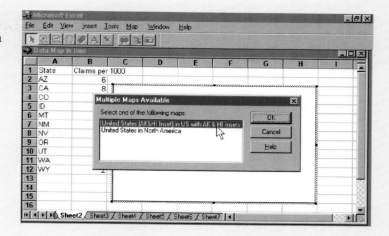

▶ The next step is in the map editing window where a map control dialog box appears.

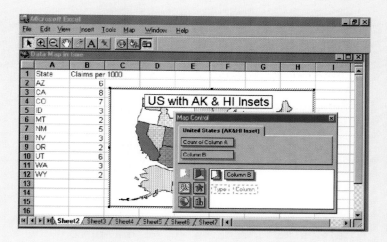

6 If you do not wish to edit the map at this time click the cancel button of the map control dialog box.

▶ The map is generated and inserted in the sheet at the selected location.

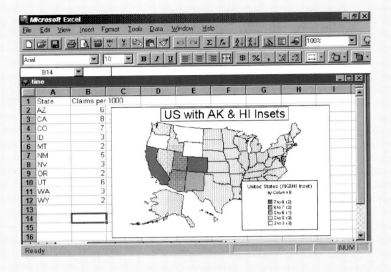

NOTE

To edit the map double-click on it and return to the map editing window. From there you can use the Map Control Box to manipulate your map display by dragging and dropping the controls within the box.

7 Before continuing to the next lesson, save the worksheet.

In the next lesson, you will get some tips on using Excel more effectively, including how to let the program check your spelling.

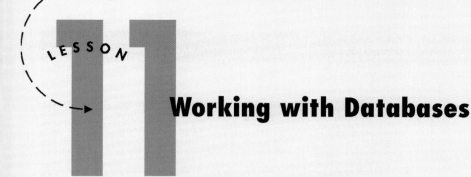

Working with Databases

If you've done the lessons thus far, you already have a basic working knowledge of Excel. You know how to lay out a worksheet, enter data and formulas, apply formats, preview and print a sheet, and save a sheet as a workbook file.

This lesson introduces some of the enhancements of Excel for Windows 95 that are designed to help you be more productive—that is, to make your work even quicker and easier—especially as you take on more complex tasks. In this lesson, you will become familiar with the Copy and Paste tools, database searches, and Pivot Tables.

Building a Table

Begin this lesson by starting Excel and building a new sheet in the default workbook, Book1. This sheet will show unit sales, by month, for three products—the Widget, the Wacker, and the Weeler.

Entering Column Headings for Field Names

The type of sheet you will build is a brief version of a typically larger *database table*. In a database table, the column headings are called *field names*. Each row of data in the table is called a *record*. You should be familiar with this type of table because it has many handy uses in Excel, which can search for and retrieve records from very large database tables, based on criteria you specify. These criteria can include field names. For example, from such a table, you could have Excel select all the sales results for the Widget product.

Start to build the table by entering its field names.

1 Click and drag to highlight the row **A1:C1**.

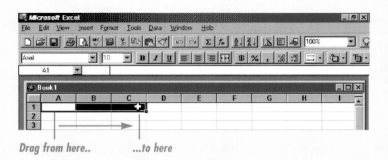

2 Type the following labels, pressing ↵ after each: **Month**, **Product**, and **Units Sold**.

Drag from here..   *...to here*

▶ These are the field names, entered as column headings. Each record will have one data item under each name.

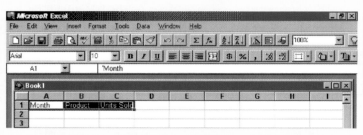

Entering the Month Labels

In this table, for each of four months, one record will be entered for each of three products. Enter the month labels now. (In this case, typing is the fastest way, because AutoFill will not generate the values in the arrangement you need.)

1 Select the range A2:A13

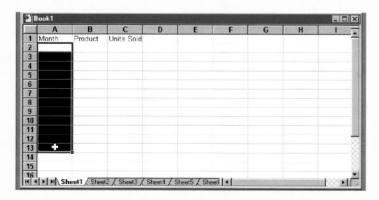

2 Type the following labels, pressing ↵ after each: **Jan**, **Jan**, **Jan**, **Feb**, **Feb**, **Feb**, **Mar**, **Mar**, **Mar**, **Apr**, **Apr**, and **Apr**.

▶ The month names should appear in the first column as shown.

Using the Copy and Paste Tools to Duplicate Product Names

In previous lessons, you used the Copy and Paste selections in the shortcut menu to duplicate data entries. Enter the product names into the table now, but use the Copy and Paste tools instead. (The equivalent command selections from the menu bar are Edit ➤ Copy and Edit ➤ Paste.)

1 Click and drag to highlight cells **B2:B4**.

2 Type the following labels, pressing ↵ after each: **Widget**, **Wacker**, and **Weeler**.

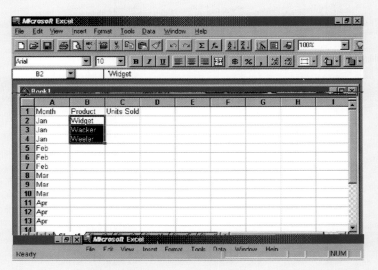

3 In the toolbar, click the **Copy** tool.

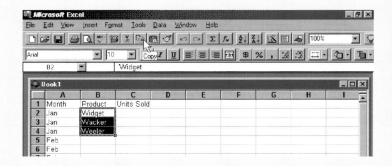

4 Click cell **B5**.

5 Click the **Paste** tool.

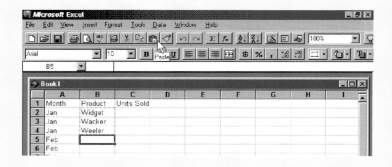

▶ The copied labels will be pasted into cells B5:B7.

6 Click cell **B8** to select it.

7 Click the **Paste** tool.

8 Click cell **B11**.

9 Click the **Paste** tool.

10 Press **Esc**.

▶ Product names should appear in all the cells shown.

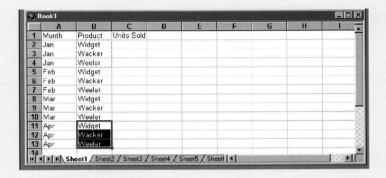

Entering the Unit Sales Data

Complete the data-entry phase of building the table by typing in the monthly unit sales for each product.

1 Click and drag to highlight the range **C2:C13**.

2 Type the following data entries, pressing ↵ after each: **117, 56, 85, 124, 69, 75, 165, 34, 68, 103, 92,** and **99**.

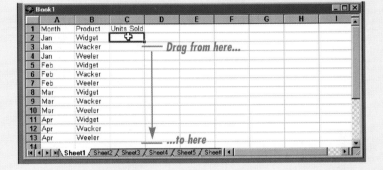

▶ The data entries in the table should be complete, as shown.

195

Saving the Sheet

Now that you have entered all the data in the table, this is an appropriate point to save your work and create a new workbook document file.

1 In the toolbar, click the **Save** tool.

▶ The Save As dialog box will appear.

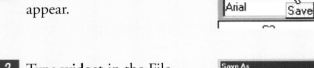

2 Type **widget** in the File name box.

3 Click **Save**.

4 Click **File ➤ Properties**

▶ The Properties dialog box will appear with the Summary tab selected.

5 Type **First Quarter Unit Sales** in the Title box.

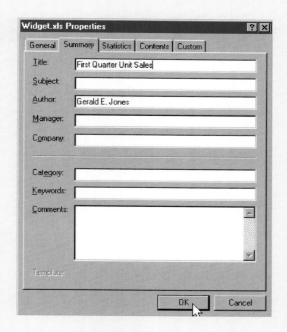

6 Click **OK**.

▶ The workbook file name will appear in the title bar of the document window.

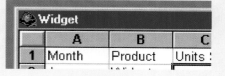

Finding Data and Records in a Database Table

Assuming that you had a much bigger table, it could be tedious to scroll through the sheet looking for a specific item. If you set up a table in which the column headings are field names, you can quickly retrieve data from it based on specific criteria. Use the table you just created to demonstrate this capability of Excel. Let's say that you wanted to know quickly how many Weelers were sold in March.

1 Click and drag to highlight the range **A1:C13** (all the cells in the table).

2 From the menu bar, select **Data ➤ Form**.

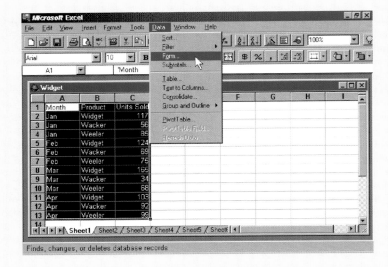

▶ A dialog box will appear showing the three fields in the first record (first row of the database table).

3 In the dialog box, click the **Criteria** button.

▶ The Month, Product, and Units Sold fields will be cleared to accept your criteria entries.

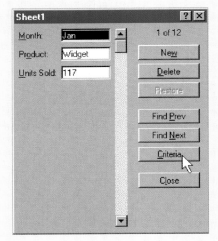

4 In the Month field, type **mar**.

5 Press **Tab** to move the cursor to the Product field.

6 Type **we**. (You need not type the whole product name—just enough to find the right matching data.)

7 Click the **Find Next** button.

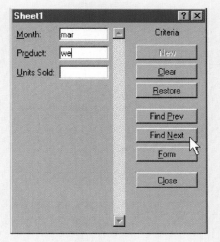

▶ The data you want will appear in the Units Sold field. The number of Weelers sold in March was 68. The number of the record containing the matching data appears in the top right of the dialog box: 9 of 12.

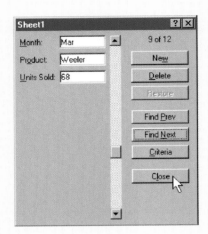

8 Click the **Close** button to close the dialog box and return to the workbook document window.

Using the PivotTable Wizard to Create a Summary Table

The layout of the database table you created is convenient for retrieving records and specific data items quickly. However, this columnar arrangement by field name is not necessarily the clearest way to report the data in a presentation. Now, use the Pivot-Table Wizard feature to create a different table layout *and* to automatically summarize sales results, both in the same quick sequence of steps.

1 With the whole table (A1:C13) still selected, select **Data ➤ PivotTable** from the menu bar.

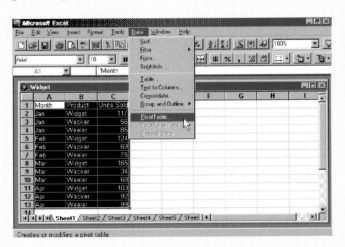

▶ The PivotTable Wizard - Step 1 of 4 dialog box will appear. Because you are using a table in the current sheet, the default option is correct.

2 In the dialog box, click the **Next** button.

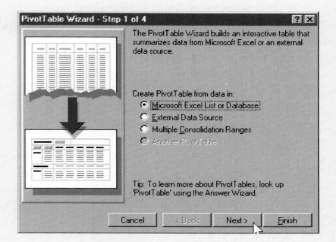

▶ The Step 2 of 4 dialog box will appear. Since you selected the table before you initiated the command, the default range reference shown here is also correct.

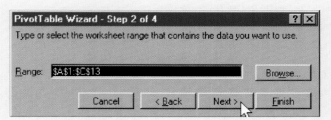

3 Click **Next**.

▶ The Step 3 of 4 dialog box will appear. Here you will define a new layout for a copy of the original table.

4 In the dialog box, drag the **Month** button into the Column portion of the sample sheet display.

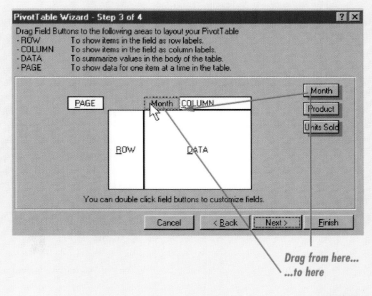

Drag from here...
...to here

5 Drag the **Product** button into the Row portion of the sample sheet.

6 Drag the **Units Sold** button into the Data portion of the sample sheet.

▶ The three field buttons should be positioned within the sample sheet as shown.

7 Click **Next**.

▶ The Step 4 of 4 dialog box will appear.

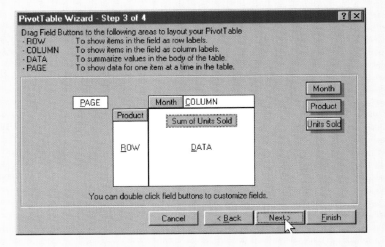

8 In the workbook document window, click cell **D1**. (If the cell is hidden by the dialog box, you can drag the title bar of the dialog box to reposition it. Or, type **d1** in the PivotTable Starting cell text box.)

9 In the dialog box, click **Finish**.

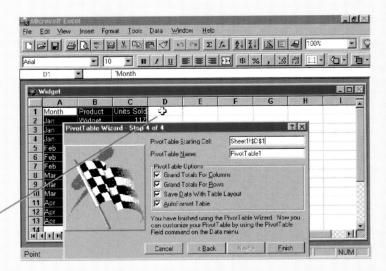

Select this cell.

A new table will be inserted into the sheet, with cell D1 as its top left corner. The columns and rows of the original table have been rearranged, and new totals have been generated for monthly and four-month total results.

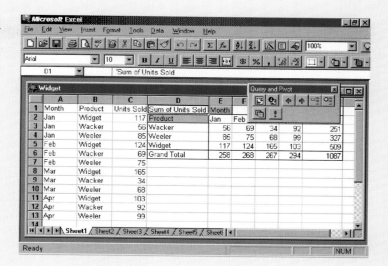

NOTE

Depending on the options you have set in View ➤ Toolbars, the Query and Pivot toolbar may appear after you select Finish. To remove the Query and Pivot Toolbar click the close control box in the upper right hand corner of the toolbar.

Manipulating a PivotTable

Notice in the sheet that the Month and Product labels in the PivotTable are displayed as buttons. You can drag these buttons to recompose the table until you see the presentation you like best. Try this now.

1 In the PivotTable, drag the **Month** button into the data area.

Drag from here...   ...to here

▶ The table will be recomposed as shown. (If your document window is not maximized, the new table will extends outside the viewing window to row 18, where a Grand Total is displayed.)

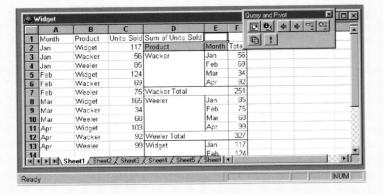

Just One More Thing...

Before you end this lesson and complete your work in this book, there is just one more thing you must do. You already know what that is. (Hint: It's a good habit that makes your work more permanent!)

Congratulations!

You have successfully completed 11 brief but comprehensive lessons on designing worksheets to solve real-world business problems. You have learned all the basic skills you need to be productive with Excel for Windows, as well as some enhanced features that can make using the program even more quick and easy!

The most difficult part—learning a new program from scratch—is behind you. As you begin to build your own worksheets, there will be opportunities to extend your proficiency. Remember that all of the features of Excel—indeed, all of the Windows applications—use the same, consistent set of controls and actions. Now that you are comfortable with these techniques, you will be able to learn new capabilities of Excel for Windows almost as soon as you discover them.

Index

Note to the Reader: **Boldfaced** numbers indicate pages where you will find the principal discussion of a topic or the definition of a term.